A Different Point of View

Can Today's Technology Reveal Hidden Secrets Contained in the Bible?

Don Bongaards P.E.

A Different Point of View

Copyright © 2021 by Don Bongaards

All rights reserved. No part of this book may be reproduced in any form or by any means—whether electronic, digital, mechanical, or otherwise—without permission in writing from the publisher, except by a reviewer, who may quote brief passages in a review.

The views and opinions expressed in this book are those of the author and do not necessarily reflect the official policy or position of Illumify Media Global.

Holy Bible, New International Version®, NIV® Copyright ©1973, 1978, 1984, 2011 by Biblica, Inc.® Used by permission. All rights reserved worldwide. New American Standard Bible®, Copyright © 1960, 1971, 1977, 1995, 2020 by The Lockman Foundation. All rights reserved. The Holy Bible, English Standard Version. ESV® Text Edition: 2016. Copyright © 2001 by Crossway Bibles, a publishing ministry of Good News Publishers. New Revised Standard Version Bible, copyright © 1989 the Division of Christian Education of the National Council of the Churches of Christ in the United States of America. Used by permission. All rights reserved.

Published by

Illumify Media Global

www.IllumifyMedia.com

"Let's bring your book to life!"

Library of Congress Control Number: 2021916135

Paperback ISBN: 978-1-955043-44-1

eBook ISBN: 978-1-955043-45-8

Cover design by Debbie Lewis

Printed in the United States of America

I dedicate this book to my daughter, Nena Harvath, and her four sons – Britt, Stewart, Johnathan, and Evan. May they live long, healthy, prosperous, and happy lives.

Contents

Introduction 1
Chapter 1—The Big Bang 9
Chapter 2—Suns, Planets, and Moons 20
Chapter 3—The Venus Connection 28
Chapter 4—Noah's Flood 34
Chapter 5—The Mustard Seed Parable 39
Chapter 6—Interstellar Travel 45
Chapter 7—A Gravity Game 54
Chapter 8—Spaceship Moon 63
Chapter 9—Are We Alone? 70
Chapter 10—God's Cosmic Puzzle 84
Chapter 11—Our Purpose 89
Chapter 12—Concluding Remarks 94
About the Author 103

Introduction

"I want to know how God created this world. I am not interested in this or that phenomenon in the spectrum of this or that element. I want to know His thoughts; the rest are details."

—Albert Einstein

WHAT IF EVERYTHING IN THE universe is there by design and not happenstance? In other words—did God design everything for a specific purpose? When looking at everything on planet Earth, it's easy to see many of things we take for granted work together in a way that reeks of design. Just think of yourself. Are humans really the result of billions of years of evolution, or are you a unique creation of God? Realizing that many people still hold on to the Darwinian theory of evolution, you might need to be made aware that that theory has long been debunked. The primary reason it was debunked is the statistical impossibility of the DNA molecule (a coded entity that determines what living things will be) and the formation of a membrane- encased, self-replicating living cell. Check it out on the Internet if you don't believe what I'm saying. Although some people believe we are the result of extraterrestrial intervention or panspermia, the impossibility of a living cell forming on its own debunks that idea as well. Therefore, it goes without saying, science has proven that there must be a God or a spiritual force in the universe that does not require physical evolution.

Since what I've just said is true, it's logical to believe that all we see is the result of design and purpose. It's also logical to believe that all we see was designed by a spiritual being or beings. My belief is that God designed all there is and created spiritual helpers called angels. I further believe that the angels wanted to have a human counterpart. Thus, the purpose of designing the universe was to create physical beings (humans that will someday become immortal with a human and spiritual coexistence) that require air, food, water, and shelter. The problem of course is that humans (or angels) needed to have a free will that could choose good or evil. If they didn't have a free will, they would just be robots (or androids). As a result, God needed to sort out those that choose good over evil. Perhaps God saw this problem when He created angels with powers like God. Lucifer and his followers come to mind.

With the above background as a starting point, I'm going to investigate all there is in a way that is counter to today's godless science. Therefore, when I see a mystery that baffles current mainstream science, or that mainstream science has misunderstood by assuming random chance, I'll take a different approach. My approach will begin by reading what God is telling us in the Bible and use modern-day scientific knowledge to explain what is probably going on. However, I'm going to apply existing laws of nature and not invoke miracles. As a design engineer I am well aware of how objects are made and how to evaluate designed objects that have already been made. Evaluating designed objects that have already been made but not knowing how they work is called reverse engineering. For instance—trying to understand how an advanced propulsion system on a crashed flying saucer works takes reverse engineering. Reverse engineering begins with a literature review to see what has been proposed in the past. In my case, the literature review begins by reading what God has said about His design.

Let me try to put what I've just said into more understandable terms. Consider that all the visible matter in the universe consists of atoms. While we know that atoms consist of protons, neutrons, electrons, and subatomic particles, we still don't know what force or forces hold them together. Moreover, we still don't really know what the protons, neutrons, electrons, and subatomic particles are made of. Therefore, why not assume they were designed by God using a technology that we currently don't understand and use reverse engineering to provide a scientific explanation—like the previously mentioned advanced propulsion system in a crashed flying saucer? Since God created Adam from the dust of the ground, it tells me that atoms can be recombined to make whatever God wants them to be. Perhaps God uses a password and the equivalent of a design file that causes the atoms to respond and assemble according to a predetermined design. Wow!—Isn't that *a different point of view?* It is a perspective that godless science avoids because it requires an advanced technology that only God may possess.

A DIFFERENT POINT OF VIEW

From my perspective it doesn't make sense for God to design atoms that don't have this recombining capability. In fact, if we assume that our immortality will include an interchangeable spiritual and physical existence recombining atoms to allow this to happen makes sense. The problem in understanding this technology—of course—is that the component parts of the atom are so small that close examination is impossible for us (even with an electron microscope). But if you are God nothing is so infinitesimally small that an intricate design is impossible. You could even imagine subatomic particles being a form of robots that are programmed to respond to a designer's wishes. The point I'm making is that although we humans don't have God's passwords and design file, we do have ways of testing the process.

As a design engineer, I've been inspired by this quote by George Bernard Shaw and later made famous by John F. Kennedy: **"Some people see things the way they are and say why. I dream of things that never were and say why not?"**

Be forewarned, this book contains radically new ideas that could revolutionize your current understanding. In preparation for the ideas I'm about to disclose, imagine yourself as a person living in the year AD 1500. An imaginative person approaches you and describes a future with jet airplanes, television, global positioning satellites, and other things we take for granted today. How would you respond? Well in modern-day times, I am that imaginative person. As I write this book, I'm almost eighty years old. I'm a retired design engineer who would like to leave behind some thoughts and ideas that will hopefully inspire current and future generations.

Whether or not you are beginning to understand where I'm going with this, I ask you to have an open mind and not be confined by preconceived notions. In any event you might at least learn some things that you've never heard or thought about before. The great scientist Albert Einstein said, *"The only thing that keeps me from learning is my education."* I think what Einstein was saying is that our education is comprised mostly of memorizing facts and opinions. In other words, education is mostly a process of teaching you *what* to think rather than teaching you *how* to think. By thinking outside the box—so to speak—Einstein changed the world by imagining what it would be like if he were traveling at the speed of light. As we all now know, our concept of time[1] has been forever changed. So don't let your education keep you from learning.

Before leaving this introduction, I want to provide two pieces of background information. The first piece of information is about the asteroid belt and gaseous planets, and the second is about our amazing Moon.

Regarding the asteroid belt between Mars and Jupiter, it contains a treasure-trove of materials including an enormous amount of water. Putting this into perspective, it's estimated that these asteroids contain 1,650,000,000,000,000,000 thousand pounds of iron; 115,500,000,000,000,000 thousand pounds of nickel; 8,250,000,000,000,000 thousand pounds of cobalt; 24,750,000,000,000 thousand pounds of platinum; plus, large quantities of other materials, such as gold, silver, copper, manganese,

---

[1] Here is a possibility regarding what we now know about time. Assume twin brothers where one brother travels near the speed of light for one year. Upon returning to Earth, he finds that his twin brother is ten years older than himself.

titanium, rare earths, silicon, and uranium. To understand what these numbers mean, if we were to build a six-inch-thick hollow iron sphere to enclose the planet Mars, we would be using only 0.011 percent of the amount of iron available. With regard to water, one asteroid in particular, Ceres, may contain about five times as much fresh water as there is on Earth. For the Ceres asteroid, a freshwater upper limit was estimated to be 430,000,000,000,000,000 thousand pounds. Now think of this. The estimated amount of helium 3 contained in the upper atmospheres of Uranus, Neptune, Saturn, and Jupiter is about 3,000,000,000,000,000 thousand pounds. When you consider 900 thousand pounds of helium 3 is enough nuclear fusion fuel to provide one year's worth of power to support the Earth's current population, you might begin to appreciate the potential of this power source and the need for mining in space: more than 3 trillion years of energy.[2]

Regarding our very strange Moon. Consider this, our moon just happens to be exactly the right size and position to support human life on planet Earth. Its presence stabilizes Earth's axis, so the Earth doesn't become gravitationally locked facing the Sun (like Venus). Moreover, through tidal interaction, the Moon prevents our oceans from becoming too salty for ocean life to exist. In other words, without our Moon human life on planet Earth could not exist.

Is our Moon just a coincidence, or is there more to the story? Does God have something to do with its existence?

I've heard it said that, scientifically speaking, our Moon shouldn't be there. Our Moon is about 238 thousand miles away

---

2 These numbers were derived from John Lewis' book *Mining the Sky* (New York: Basic Books 1997).

from us and is currently receding from the Earth at about 1.6 inches per year (please excuse my avoidance of the metric system at this point). This recession is a result of gravitational interaction that is caused by the motion of tides on Earth. When, or if, the Moon was closer to the Earth, the gravitational and tidal effects would have been quite different.

A recent Science Channel program explained that a large planet-sized object collided with the Earth about 4 billion years ago. The Earth's gravity pulled the heavier elements away from the debris, thus making the remaining debris only 60 percent as dense as the Earth. After the collision, the debris coalesced to form a spherical object, our Moon, which traveled in an orbit about fourteen thousand miles from the Earth. Because of tidal interactions, the Moon has since receded to the point where it is now. Using this impact model, the Science Channel once again had a scientific spokesperson confidently and all-knowingly pronounce that this is how the Moon was formed and why it is where it is today. As I see it, this rational is irrational. Let me explain. My calculations show that the Moon's gravitational interaction with the Earth would be 295 times stronger if it were fourteen thousand miles from Earth's surface. What do you think would happen on Earth if the Moon was orbiting only a few thousand miles away rather than its current 238 thousand miles? Imagine its effect on Earth's spin rate, atmosphere, and ocean tides.

Whatever you believe to be the origin of the Moon, it does have some pretty unusual and amazing characteristics. As mentioned above, it's exactly the right size, it's located in exactly the right place, and it exists at exactly the right time in human history. It's almost as if it had been deliberately placed there for our benefit.

If you were to examine the Moon based upon a preconceived notion (current mainstream scientific thinking) of how planetary bodies must have been formed, you would probably be quite surprised. Rather than gravity forming heavier elements at its core, we find an abundance of refractory elements like titanium on its surface. Moreover, seismic testing on the Moon revealed that it acted more like it was hollow rather than being a homogeneous sphere.

As a final note regarding the Moon, in the History Channel's series *Ancient Aliens,* an episode about the Moon provided compelling evidence (including books by reputable scientists) to support the idea that the Moon might be a manmade spacecraft. Of course, since the Ancient Alien theme is that Earth has been visited by aliens from another solar system, the source of the Moon spacecraft, in their opinion is the result of an alien creation. Since aliens cannot exist without themselves being created by God, there might be another logical explanation that I'll provide as you continue to read this book.

Chapter 1—The Big Bang

"Science without religion is lame, religion without science is blind."
—Albert Einstein

THE SCIENCE CHANNEL AIRED A program called *An Introduction to the Universe*. The program was presented in the words of the late Stephen Hawking and subtitled **as *the story of everything*.** As most of you may know, Stephen Hawking was regarded by many in the scientific community to be the Einstein of recent times.

The program began with an explanation for how the universe came into existence. At first there was a very small atom-sized entity called a singularity, and time and space as we know it did not exist. Then the singularity exploded, and within a trillionth of a second it was the size of an orange. In one hundred seconds it expanded to a diameter that was billions of miles across. In ten minutes it was thousands of light-years in diameter. Contained in the subatomic, radiated particles from the explosion were matter and anti-matter, which annihilated each other when they came into contact. Luckily for us, according to Hawking, an imbalance of one in one billion particles was matter that survived the blast. Three hundred and thirty-thousand years later, a subatomic particle fog lifted and became visible as hydrogen atoms. At that point, gravitational attraction and naturally occurring spatial imperfections took over and caused the hydrogen particles to cluster together. As this clustering took place, a fusion reaction occurred as the impacting forces of the hydrogen atoms reached a temperature of 10 million degrees, thus forming stars like our sun. At the center of these stars, the hydrogen atoms fused to form the element helium. Because of tremendous gravitational forces, the temperature further increased to cause additional fusion reactions of the helium atoms, which resulted in the formation of carbon. Finally, the carbon atoms fused to form iron atoms. Because the iron atoms could not continue the fusion process, the stars' fuel supply ran out and they began to collapse in on themselves and cause an explosion—a supernova. As the stars collapsed, temperatures were so high the iron atoms began to fuse together. As a result, all the heavier elements that currently exist were created and new stars and solar systems began to form from the exploded debris. These solar systems were also affected by gravitational attraction and their clustering resulted in galaxies. At the center of each galaxy is an unrestrained gravitational collapse that resulted in what is called a gigantic "black hole," where the gravitational attraction is so great that even light cannot escape. Within one of the billions of galaxies that were formed, we find an instance where a planet called Earth had the mysterious special characteristics needed to form organic, carbon-based life. Some of that life mysteriously developed into a special type that had the ability to contemplate what caused the universe and everything in it.

If the above description of the formation of the universe and human life isn't mind boggling enough, the wonders and mysteries of the universe continue even further. Scientists now say that the universe is not only expanding but that the expansion is accelerating. This scientific finding runs counter to intuition, which would predict a slowing down and even a contraction of the universe as a result of gravitational attraction. What this finding implies is that a mysterious substance called "dark energy" is causing the acceleration. If that were not strange enough, other observations of galactic motion infer that another substance called "dark matter" must also exist. When working out the cosmic math, scientists have concluded that 70 percent of the universe is dark energy and 25 percent is dark matter. Thus, only 5 percent of the universe is matter which is visible to our current detection devices. Because we can see with our telescopes exploding stars in our own Milky Way galaxy and in other galaxies, we can infer that stars and their solar systems have a finite life. If stars have a finite life, and their exploding debris is insufficient to form new stars, it's likely that the universe could eventually burn up and become littered with black holes. If the dark energy that scientists claim is driving the universe apart runs out of steam, the universe could reverse its expansion and collapse in upon itself due to gravity—a process that Hawking calls the Big Crunch. If this were to happen, the universe could return to something like the Hawking singularity and explode again in a never-ending cycle of universe recreations.

In his narrative, Hawking poses the question that he is often asked, is there a designer? His answer is "not necessarily so," and his reasoning is that there may have been an infinite number of other universes (multiverses), and only one may have allowed Earth's coincidences to happen. Apparently Hawking understood the mathematical impossibilities of all these miracles working out just right, and an "infinite number of universes" argument tends to counteract these impossibilities!

One other point worth mentioning is Hawking's claim that an asteroid is likely to hit planet Earth sometime in the future and wipe out most of Earth's life-forms. He points to the asteroid that hit the Yucatan Peninsula 65 million years ago and supposedly wiped out the dinosaurs as evidence that it will probably happen again. Because of this possibility, Hawking warned that humans need to develop a capability for living on Mars and eventually interstellar migration.

There you have it, **"the story of everything,"** as told by a one of the most respected scientists of our time.

After reading what Hawking and the mainstream scientific community are saying, I'm struck by the fact that no credit is given to God. When Hawking was confronted by the question "is there a designer," he immediately jumped to the idea of multi universes. Although mainstream scientists are doing their best to keep from invoking God in their studies, their supposed scientifically based solutions are causing them anguish to the point of being absurd.

As a skeptic I try to read between the lines of what mainstream science is telling us. In other words, I try to discern fact from fiction using the idea that everything in the universe is there by design and not random happenstance. What I see is a huge universe and our small planet Earth as having been designed that way for a purpose.

CHAPTER 1—THE BIG BANG

So what is this mysterious singularity? What are black holes? What is dark energy and dark matter? What causes gravity? How did hydrogen mysteriously form? None of these things are explained in Hawking's story of everything. Since everything that Hawking is saying is scientific speculation (story telling) with scientific attributes that make it sound authoritative, please allow me to do some speculating of my own.

Hawking claims that in ten minutes after the big bang, matter and antimatter were thousands of light-years from the originating singularity. Does this mean that matter had traveled faster than the speed of light, or does it mean that the speed of light was faster at this early point in time? Hmm . . . interesting!

As you may know, the speed of light is considered to be a constant and much of what we assume for determining distance and age is dependent on this assumption. Is there reason to believe that the speed of light may have been much faster at the beginning of time? In fact, there is scientific evidence that supports this idea.[3] If true, then the idea of the universe expanding and accelerating as a result of dark energy might be wrong, and scientists could be totally misled when determining distances and age.

My speculation about the origin of the universe begins with Christ saying, **"I am the light of the world."** By taking these words literally, let's consider that God has control of the

---

3   For example, since spiral galaxies should spin at the same rate based upon orbital mechanics, one would expect to see distant galaxies spinning slower than closer galaxies if the speed of light was always constant. However, this is not the case. The Hubble telescope shows a similar spin rate for a galaxy 100 million light-years away as it does for one that is 10 million light-years away.

various natural laws of light. In this sense God is capable of controlling the speed of light and its influence upon time and matter/mass.

Let's begin by defining three known natural laws governing light. The first law is that matter/mass cannot travel faster than the speed of light. The second law is that time slows down as we approach the speed of light (perhaps zero time at the speed of light). The third law is that matter/mass and energy are defined according to Einstein's equation $E=mc^2$ where matter/mass (m) and energy (E) are interchangeable according to the speed of light (c). Could it be that the previously mentioned unknowns (a singularity, black holes, dark energy and matter, gravity, and hydrogen atoms) can be explained using these known laws of nature and a changing speed of light? Besides, since God created these laws, why would He violate them when creating the universe. In fact, one could ask the reverse question: why did God create these laws in the first place if they didn't serve a purpose?

Beginning with the idea that mass and energy are interchangeable ($E=mc^2$) according to the speed of light. What if the speed of light was infinite at the beginning of time and God began reducing it? As a result, energy might begin a process of collapsing in upon itself in the form of an implosion. At some point during this implosion there could be a reversal—an explosion where energy becomes a form of matter/mass. For all intents and purposes let's call the reversal point a "singularity." Keep in mind, however, that in my thought experiment God is continuing to reduce the speed of light. Therefore, as I see it the resulting speed of the exploding matter/mass is limited by the reducing speed of light. Since time is assumed to be zero when traveling at the speed of light, the originating matter/mass would exist at a different time zero than subsequent exploding matter/mass. Thus, it's my opinion that more than one time zero cannot coexist. If so, a tremendous force might be created to neutralize this differential time incompatibility. Let's call it a black hole. During this explosive process it's conceivable that a second implosion and explosion takes place. During the second explosion fragments of the originating black hole are scattered throughout space and become galaxies. Surrounding these galaxies are smaller black hole fragments that create hydrogen atoms that form suns. After running out of fuel for nuclear fusion reactions, some of the larger suns (about ten times larger than our Sun) then explode as supernovae. In the exploding debris from the supernovae, new solar systems that contain planets like Earth are formed.

What I've just described is an unsubstantiated hypothesis, a thought experiment based upon God having control over the speed of light. Moreover, keep in mind that during the process I've just described the speed of light is continually decreasing, thus giving the illusion of an expanding and accelerating universe without the need of dark energy and matter. Of course, the idea of smaller and smaller black hole fragments also explains the source of gravity.

Does my hypothesis also explain atoms? As we know, at the center of each atom are protons and neutrons. Surrounding the protons and neutrons are electrons and subatomic particles. Since mainstream science has yet to provide a reasonable explanation for the force that holds atoms together, my explanation begins with subatomic black holes being responsible for this force. Since I believe God controls the speed of light, it's conceivable that if black holes are a "speed of light dependent" phenomena, that can be controlled, imagine what this could mean. Can atoms become neutralized and reassembled according to a preconceived design? How about Adam being created from the atoms contained in the dust of the ground?

So, there you have it, my hypothesis (thought experiment) regarding an alternative to Stephen Hawking's story of everything. In case you haven't noticed, my story of everything also explains how it all began. In other words who or what started it in the first place.

This gets me back to the basis for this book: that God designed everything for a purpose. If so, what would be God's purpose for a faster speed of light at the beginning of time and a time domain differential being the source that binds matter/mass together? Well, if God can control light, He can also neutralize time-light dependent black holes in a way that allows atoms to be reassembled according to a preconceived design like a human. If true, I can imagine that in our immortal afterlife we could choose to exist as either a spiritual being or a human being.

To help support my thinking, before retiring as an engineer I was continually interested in inventing things that improve or replace existing products, devices, processes, or even human circumstances. Since retirement I've continued inventing things and exploring new ideas as a hobby (like writing this book). Recently one of my grandsons got me interested in 3D printing. With my newly acquired printing machine I'm now able to draw 3D objects on my computer and reproduce these objects by sending a file to the printer. While watching this amazing machine transform my design into a real object, it occurred to me that, on a much more advanced scale, God might have created Adam from dust atoms using a preconceived design and a password to reconstruct dust atoms into His design. In this case I can imagine God creating DNA molecules with coded information needed to produce all kinds of living things. Further along this line of thinking, what if our immortal existence consists of an interchangeable spiritual and human body. I can imagine atoms in the air or dust from the ground being used as ingredients for this transformation. Think of the transporter used in *Star Trek*.

I can't mathematically or experimentally prove everything I've said so far, but that doesn't mean that other scientists or mathematicians won't find a way. After all, Einstein's theory that gravity bends light was proven during an eclipse of the sun. In any case, I think you will agree that my thinking has a biblical and scientific basis that should cause some doubt about what we are being told by a godless mainstream scientific community. While I believe that many scientists do believe in God, they avoid using a "predesigned by God" viewpoint in their research because it could jeopardize their careers and possibly their funding. Since I'm retired, my career and funding is not an issue with me. I am concerned, however, about ridicule—even after my death. On the other hand, perhaps what I've said so far, and what I'm going to say in this book, might stimulate others to travel "outside the box" that's possibly confining their thinking. If so, it might advance our scientific understanding and cause non-believers to reconsider the truth of what the Bible is trying to tell us.

In concluding this chapter, I want to address Hawking's comments about the need for interstellar travel and living on Mars (I assume because of overpopulation). Considering that our

A DIFFERENT POINT OF VIEW

nearest solar system—Alpha Centauri—is about four light-years away (today's light speed is 186,000 miles per second), even with our most advanced propulsion systems it would take us many thousands of years to get there. Even then—what reason would humans have for going there, if there were no known earthlike planets waiting for them? In essence it would be a suicide mission.

By the way, if you inquire about interstellar travel on the Internet, you'll find that Godless science is desperately trying to solve this problem with ideas that I would call grasping for straws. These ideas range from worm holes, solar kites, ion propulsion, altering space in the form of a bubble around the spacecraft, and matter-antimatter propulsion. On the other hand, I have an idea that may or may not work. As I see it, the problem is not whether we can reach the speed required to make interstellar travel practical. It's the amount of on-board fuel we will need. If we were to construct enough Apollo/Saturn rockets—powered by helium 3 nuclear fusion energy and water (that's separated into hydrogen and oxygen fuel)—we can create enough acceleration to eventually reach light speed. However, when you do the math, the water fuel (and even the nuclear fusion fuel) required is enormous. When faced with this reality, it suddenly occurred to me that the exhaust from hydrogen/oxygen fueled Apollo/Saturn rockets is water vapor that might be captured and recycled. Thus, the amount of water fuel needed at takeoff could be minimal. Since nuclear fusion creates ten times more energy than it consumes, the energy part of the equation would be limited by the amount of lightweight helium-3 fuel (gathered from the upper atmospheres of the gaseous planets) that could be frozen and carried on board. Well, what I'm saying must be wrong since—from what I'm finding—no one else has thought of it. On the other hand, it does seem logical to me, and my preliminary calculations and logic show it to be feasible.

Again, I believe Hawking's claim that we humans should eventually live on Mars is absurd, especially when building huge rotating satellite[4] habitats is the most logical answer to Hawking's concern for overpopulation and fear of asteroids. How is it that so many brilliant minds—like Hawking's—can come to so many irrational conclusions?

Contrary to what I've said so far, I do consider some of the aspects of Hawking's description of events leading up to the formation of planet Earth and living organisms to be quite logical—especially having a beginning (e.g., Genesis 1:1). In fact, the formation of new suns and solar systems from supernovae explosions (an observed phenomena) has caused me to give some thought to planet and moon formation—especially about our planet Earth and Moon. When I try to get specific scientific information about planet and moon formation, I find that godless science has again provided unsubstantiated opinions (stories with some scientific basis). Well, since this is open to debate, I'll give it a shot in the next chapter.

---

4   If the satellite habitat were a rotating cylinder, the rotation could simulate gravity on the inside surface as a result of centrifugal force—like tying a ball at the end of a string and spinning it around.

Chapter 2—Suns, Planets, and Moons

"For nothing is hidden that will not be made manifest, nor is anything secret that will not be known and come to light."

—Luke 8:17 ESV

MY FORTHCOMING RENDITION OF HOW suns, planets, and moons are formed is based upon my previously mentioned assumption that everything created by God is by design. By making this assumption, much of what has baffled mainstream science might begin to make sense. So, as I see it, by rejecting the intervention of God, mainstream science has become unable to understand what is really going on. In other words, if mainstream scientists were to assume that everything in the universe is there by design, a totally new way of thinking could emerge. Rather than assuming randomness, a new approach would be to ask the question how would I design the universe if I were God?

CHAPTER 2—SUNS, PLANETS, AND MOONS

In the last chapter we saw how Stephen Hawking stated a supernova (a gigantic exploding sun) created our solar system. As I see it, the explosion consisted mainly of hydrogen with lesser amounts of each element according to their mass. So in the exploding mass, a gravitational collapse (or maybe something else like a black hole) causes hydrogen to fuse and make helium (our sun) with the remaining elements being flung into space. My guess is that these elements become spinning near-homogeneous molten plasma clumps that surround black holes and eventually coalesce into planets and moons of varying sizes and orbit at varying distances around the newly formed sun. If true, pre-planets might spin at a high rate of speed (obviously this is just a guess). Although gravity will try to form these supposedly homogeneous plasma clumps into a spherical shape, centrifugal forces (angular momentum) might at first dominate gravity. In other words, a high spin rate will cause centrifugal forces to dominate gravitational forces. So if we assume a high spin rate, a pre-planet's shape would become elliptical. In other words, it would resemble an iconic flying saucer. Also, since its beginning state might have been a homogeneous mixture of heavy and light elements, centrifugal forces would act to separate these elements (like a centrifuge). As a result, heavy elements like iron would be thrust toward the perimeter of the elliptical entity, with the lighter elements being left behind. Since lighter elements are comprised of gasses like hydrogen and helium, a gaseous void would tend to form at the center of the elliptical entity. In some cases, the heavy elements might become satellite (moon) material that orbits the equator of the ellipse.[5]

During this redistribution process, however, the heavy elements would eventually cause the spin rate of the ellipse to slow down (like when an ice skater extends his or her arms after spinning at a high rate). As a result, gravitational forces will eventually cause the elliptical entity to become a sphere with a hollow gas filled center. Also, during the redistribution process the heavy, hot elements would tend to cool by radiating heat into space and become reacted compounds like iron oxide. Because of the slowing spin rate, the heavy elements and reacted compounds would tend to gravitationally move toward the center of the spherical mass. Since cooling (radiation to space) and solidification would have preceded his inward movement, the centrally located gasses would be restricted/blocked in their attempt to migrate to the outer surface. Moreover, other cooled and orbiting elements and compounds would tend to bombard the surface and form craters or remain in orbit as moons. The question at this point, would be whether or not the gas-filled central void is completely displaced or remains a gas-filled void. With regard to the bombardment of the surface of the pre-planet entity, it's conceivable that the rotational axis of the resulting sphere would swing wildly due to impacting forces and a changing center of mass. This would cause crater impacts to appear somewhat uniformly distributed on the surface.

---

5   The moons that currently exist in our solar system are small relative to the size of the planets they orbit. This is not true for Earth's Moon which also continually changes orbit due to tidal/gravitational interaction.

So what does this description of planet and moon formation have to do with the formation of Earth and its Moon? Well, with regard to the early version of planet Earth, the center may or may not have been hollow. However, if it isn't hollow, molten iron oxide might still be circulating (causing our magnetic field), and a hydrogen fusion sun-like entity might have formed at the gravitationally neutral center. Since hydrogen and oxygen may have reacted during the cooldown timeframe to form water, and nitrogen reacting with hydrogen to form ammonia, the dominant gas that may have migrated to form the surface atmosphere might have been mostly carbon dioxide. As far as our Moon is concerned, its smaller mass might have left a hollow gas-filled center with a negligible surface atmosphere. Since hydrogen and oxygen might have combined to form water, it's conceivable that water might have collected on the inner surface of our Moon (if it is indeed hollow). Whether or not a mini sun might have formed at our Moon's gravity neutral center is a matter of further speculation. By the way, at this point I'm treating the formation of our Moon as a mini planet that's orbiting the Sun or orbiting one of the gaseous planets and not orbiting our Earth.

For the gaseous planets like Jupiter, Saturn, Uranus, and Neptune it's conceivable that a sun-like fusion reaction occurred at their centers and kept the returning heavy elements molten or re-melted them, thus, allowing lightweight gasses like helium 3 to find a pathway through the liquid medium and dominate their upper atmospheres. Moreover, some clusters of matter could have remained in orbit to form moons. On the other hand, because of the size and mass of these gaseous planets their centrifugal forces (as result of their spinning) might not have overcome the gravitational forces. My rational here comes from the fact that the moons surrounding the gaseous planets are generally covered with ice or ammonia, and because they **are** gaseous planets it tells me that gravity caused the heavy elements to reach their centers while the gaseous elements remained on their surfaces.

On a side note, these ideas about the formation of the gaseous planets caused me to believe Earth's moon might have originated as one of Jupiter's moons. Strangely all the moons in our solar system have a density similar to Earth's moon except for Jupiter's moon Lo, which is slightly denser but nowhere near as dense as the solid planets: Earth, Mars, Venus, and Mercury. If our Moon was once one of Jupiter's moons, it begs the question: why doesn't our Moon have an icy surface, since Europa, one of Jupiter's moons that's of similar size and mass, and has an icy surface? Then it struck me. If our Moon was transformed into a spacecraft, it would need to accelerate to leave Jupiter's orbit. Once near Earth's orbit the ice would melt and become steam in the vacuum of space (since water boils in a vacuum). And, because of the spacecraft Moon's acceleration, the steam could separate and be left behind and possibly become a comet (or comets). In case you're rolling your eyes at my spacecraft Moon assertion, I'll explain later. I believe you will be very much surprised.

Back to the idea that the hydrogen gas from a supernova explosion probably gravitationally collapsed to form our sun—as stated by Steven Hawking. Is that all there is to it? I wondered. Being curious, I decided to examine the agreed-upon mass of our Sun based upon its size and supposed composition (hydrogen). Let's begin with the volume of our Sun:

$V_{olume} = 4/3 \times \pi \times r_{adius}^3$

Since r = 695,700,000 meters, V = 1.41 × 10²⁷ cubic meters and the density of a cubic meter of hydrogen at Earth's atmospheric pressure/temperature = 0.08988 kgs/m³, and the published mass of our Sun = 1.9885 × 10³⁰ kilograms, then when we multiply 0.08988 kgs/m³ × 1.41 × 10²⁷ m³ we get 1.24 × 10²⁶ kilograms as the mass of the sun—not the published 1.9885 × 10³⁰ kilograms. Therefore, we need to increase the hydrogen density to result in the published mass. Here is the result:(1.9885 × 10³⁰ / 1.24 × 10²⁶) × 0.08988 = 1,411 kgs/m³

Although the above calculation assumes an average hydrogen density, I can't imagine a cubic meter of hydrogen having a mass of more than a thousand kilograms. While I might have overlooked something here it does seem strange. Since our Sun is not very big when compared to other suns in the universe, the thousand kilograms per cubic meter of hydrogen becomes even stranger. For instance, the largest sun in the universe is estimated to have a radius 2,600 times greater than our Sun.

So what is the point I'm trying to make? How about each sun (or star) having black holes at their centers? Rather than assume black holes, mainstream science has calculated the percentage of helium that could have been formed over billions of years with the remaining percentage being unreacted hydrogen and a small percentage of other elements. As a result, they have accepted the idea that hydrogen or helium can be compressed to thousands of kilograms per cubic meter!

If I'm right about black holes being the source of gravity, I wouldn't be surprised to find that all of our planets also formed around black holes. With regard to moon formation, what if black holes resulted in mini suns at their hollow centers? This is an important point that I will be expounding later. With regard to our planet Earth having a carbon dioxide atmosphere, it's conceivable that Earth's surface temperature would become hot as a result of a greenhouse effect. Moreover, Earth's spin rate might have slowed to a crawl. If so, the net result of our early Earth might have been similar to what exists with our sister planet Venus today.

As far as the Earth and Moon being bombarded with elements and reacted compounds to form craters, Earth's surface would eventually smooth out as a result of a significantly higher gravitational force (a known scientific process called creep).

At this point you may still be rolling your eyes in disbelief. After all, I'm not a trained cosmologist. ***What does he know?*** you might be asking yourself. Well, as you can see from Stephen Hawking's description of how the universe was formed without invoking God as the Creator, there's plenty of room for a minority opinion that assumes design by God. Besides, as you will see, as we move on, my opinion of how planet Earth was formed has some scientific (centrifugal force) and biblical (book of Genesis) backing; and as I previously mentioned, a hollow Moon also has scientific backing from seismic testing. Both Earth and Moon have heavy elements on their surface, which if formed by gravity alone—without a beginning centrifugal force effect—wouldn't make sense because the heavy elements essential to human existence would have sunk toward a molten center (probably what happened during the formation of the gaseous planets). Moreover, it seems strange that our Moon is much less dense than our Earth! Interestingly, my calculations show that if I remove a 1,500-mile diameter (based upon a dimension described in the book of Revelation) sphere from the Moon's center, it's new density would be similar to planet Earth. More on this later.

    Therefore, the pre-terraformed Earth (based on the book of Genesis account of Earth's creation) may have looked like Venus today. Venus is considered Earth's sister planet because of its similar size and density. Its surface temperature is about 900 degrees Fahrenheit, it has a mostly carbon dioxide atmosphere, and its spin cycle is 243 Earth days. Strangely though, Venus doesn't have a moon. If planet Earth was once like Venus before it was terraformed (transformed into the attributes of planet Earth), one might ask, did God create Venus-like planets throughout the universe that are waiting for us to terraform them during our immortal existence? If so, does our Moon have something to do with terraforming, and can Venus be terraformed? Stay tuned as I examine this possibility.

Chapter 3—The Venus Connection

"Ask and it will be given to you; seek and you will find; knock and the door will be opened to you."

—Mathew 7:7 NIV

MANY OF THE THOUGHTS AND ideas that have come to my mind while doing research for this book have surprised me. As Louis Pasteur once said more than a century ago, **"Chance favors the prepared mind."** By this he meant that sudden flashes of insight don't just happen. They are the products of preparation.

You might think some of the things I wrote in the last chapter are outrageous. Terraforming Venus is an especially far out idea, but, as you will see, I believe it reflects what God is trying to tell us in the Bible—specifically with regard to the six days of creation.

To begin, let me explain why I'm investigating the possibility of terraforming Venus? To my way of thinking, we, during our immortal existence, will terraform earthlike planets throughout the universe. (I'll provide biblical support of why this makes sense later.) This idea explains why our planet is so small and the universe is so large.

As previously stated, our sister planet, Venus, seemed like a good candidate to begin this investigation. Why? Because random happenings are not part of God's plan. I believe Venus was placed where it is by design and not happenstance. I also believe that is true for the other planets and moons in our solar system for other reasons, but the characteristics of Venus became of particular interest to me from a terraforming standpoint. It also became of interest to me because, as described in the previous chapter, our planet Earth was probably very much like Venus before it was terraformed in six days. Since Earth has a moon and Venus does not, it's logical to assume that our Moon might have had something to do with Earth's terraforming process.

Before trying to imagine ways to terraform Venus, I saw a television episode of *Cosmos: A Personal Voyage*—a thirteen-part, 1980 television series presented by Carl Sagan—called "Heaven and Hell." At one point Sagan proposed a way to cool Venus with a Sun-blocking shield that would be four times the diameter of Venus and be located in what's called the Lagrange point. The Lagrange point is a location in space where the gravitational forces of two large bodies, such as Earth and the Moon and the Sun and the Moon are equal. Although a functional manmade object the size of Carl Sagan's proposed sun-blocking shield would, in my opinion, be impossible to create, it occurred to me that perhaps an earth-sized moon could cool early Earth or Venus if it were a maneuverable spacecraft. If a moon-sized spacecraft

A DIFFERENT POINT OF VIEW

could through several flybys act like a gravitational tugboat and set Venus on a twenty-four-hour spin rate (as previously mentioned Venus' current spin rate is 243 Earth days) and position it close to Earth's orbit, it might be able to cool Venus enough to cause what I believe could be a miraculous transformation that might be part of God's plan.

Are you starting to see where I'm going with this? In the previous chapter I postulated that planet Earth might have once had much the same attributes as Venus before it was terraformed—a very hot, carbon dioxide–rich atmosphere; a slow rotational speed; and a circular orbit. With this thought in mind, what if our Moon was once a "spacecraft" that blocked the Sun for a predetermined length of time and caused our pre-terraformed Earth to cool. But that's not all folks. Some amazing things might have also happened.

During the cool-down period, hydrogen might act to transform the carbon dioxide–rich atmosphere into water and methane (the Sabatier reaction):

$$CO_2 + 4H_2 \xrightarrow{400°C\ heat/pressure} 2H_2O + CH_4$$

The source of hydrogen might have been the result of Earth's or Venus' initial formation where water and ammonia might have become trapped beneath the planet's surface. My speculation is that during the cool-down period, the surface of a pre-earthlike planet like Venus will separate to form a subsurface void (like when a hard-boiled egg is put into ice water the shell separates from the egg white inside). As a result, the heavy carbon dioxide in the atmosphere could gravitationally sink into this void and react with hydrogen to form water and methane. The hydrogen might have come from depressurized ammonia into nitrogen and hydrogen ($3NH_3 > N_2 + 3H_2$) at 500°C. During this reaction, the nitrogen gas could have combined with oxygen (derived from depressurized high temperature water and/or other sources) to form a new transparent atmosphere. Some surface water might also result from seepage from the newly formed subsurface water. Regarding the methane, it likely could have formed subsurface natural gas, oil, and coal over time.

Is it possible that Venus could become earthlike during a cool-down cycle? Is it possible that perhaps our planet Earth might have been like Venus at an earlier time and that our Moon was capable of cooling it? We'll talk later about Jupiter's earth-sized moon Europa that might be available to experiment with Venus later.

Ok, I get it. You're probably still rolling your eyes in disbelief. Be that as it may, let me explain my thoughts on this subject from a biblical perspective.

Let's begin with the Sun and Moon appearing on the fourth day of creation. Consider this. On the *first day* God said, **"let there be light."** This would happen on the Earth's surface when an opaque carbon dioxide-carbon monoxide-sulfur dioxide-methane atmosphere was removed and replaced by a transparent oxygen-nitrogen atmosphere. At this point a previously unseen light, from Earth's surface, would be a result of the Sun's glow around a stationary eclipsing Moon at the Lagrange point. God also separated daylight from nighttime on the first day when creating Earth's twenty-four-hour rotation. This could mean that the brighter light emanating from the eclipsing Sun-Moon glow would be seen for only about half of the twenty-four-hour rotation and the stars during the second half.

On the *second day* God separated the waters from the surface and subsurface. (Remember the water would have formed in the subsurface void as a result of **the Sabatier reaction** with some water reaching Earth's surface to form shallow seas.)

On the *third day* God created dry land and land-based vegetation. Dry land would result from shrinkage (wrinkling) of the planet's surface because of thermal contraction while cooling, and the creation of vegetation would have been a logical next step (more on how this step might have happened later).

On the *fourth day* God created two great lights. This would be the result of re-positioning the Sun-eclipsing moon to its current orbit around the Earth and thus exposing the full face of the Sun during the day and the reflection of the Sun's light off the Moon at night. Now the actions God took on the fourth day suddenly make sense. It makes sense because without the Sun being in place during day one, the Earth would not be in orbit around it, and Earth's surface would have been frozen to a point that surface water could not exist, and vegetation could not grow.

Finally, regarding the possibility of a subsurface void forming during the cool-down phase of terraforming Venus, consider this. Today's computer technology can make detailed time-dependent analysis of structural and fluid interactions. (It's called finite element structural and fluid analysis.) Although current computer models are trying to predict climate change, they are currently totally inadequate with regard to the many variables involved. However, this is more a result of computer speed and process time than it is with knowing the interacting variables. Advancements in computer process speed and programming, however, will more than likely overcome this deficiency. When this happens, it may be possible to analyze planet Earth's formation from the beginning of its existence. For instance, we can start with Earth being in a spinning and molten state and follow its development to our present time. This analysis would require varying many parameters (possibly thousands of reruns/iterations) to ultimately match known parameters from seismic testing, mineral deposits, and observed variants on Earth's surface (like mountain formation and the oceanic trench that encircles the Earth). When the analysis is complete, further analysis might include a Venus scenario. If this is done, it could create a deliberate, time-dependent cooling sequence where a subterranean gap might be formed, and the sequence of events that I've described might follow. If the results of such an analysis were positive, it would provide the incentive for creating a moon-sized spacecraft to prove the hypothesis. In other words, attempting to terraform Venus (or a similar planet in another solar system) without prior analysis wouldn't make sense.

So while you may or may not agree with my thinking, it does make the Genesis account of light on day one, and the Sun/Moon light on day four rational and in accord with the laws of nature. It also makes the six days of creation more understandable. By the way, did you notice the formation of subterranean water? Is this where Noah's flood water came from?

Chapter 4—Noah's Flood

"In the six hundredth year of Noah's life in the second month, on the seventeenth day of the month, on the same day all the fountains of the great deep burst open, and the floodgates of the sky were opened."

—**Genesis 7:11** NASB

As you may recall from reading the last chapter, if planet Earth was originally like Venus before terraforming, a large amount of subterranean water might have been formed by hydrogen reacting with carbon dioxide (the Sabatier reaction). As a result, this subterranean water could have become the source of Noah's flood. If so, it tends to support my contention that Earth was once like Venus before terraforming. Here is further evidence that supports this idea.

In his book, ***In the Beginning,*** MIT physicist Dr. Walt Brown theorizes that before the global flood there was a subterranean ocean about ten miles beneath Earth's crust. Brown's theory is based upon the Bible's Genesis account.

In 1962 Soviet researchers began drilling the deepest hole in Earth's upper crust—the Kola Superdeep Borehole. By 1994 they stopped drilling at a depth of 7.5 miles, which was 1.7 miles short of their intended goal. Contrary to scientific opinion at that time, they didn't find the transition from granite to basalt between two to four miles of depth that was predicted by seismic testing. Even more surprising was the discovery of water. Another unexpected find was a menagerie of fossils as deep as 4.2 miles, and despite the harsh environment of heat and pressure their microscopic remains were remarkably intact. The researchers were also surprised at how quickly the temperatures rose as the borehole deepened. At the 7.5-mile depth the drill bit began to reach its maximum heat tolerance. Instead of the predicted temperature of about 210 degrees Fahrenheit, it was instead 355 degrees Fahrenheit. At that temperature and pressure the rocks began to act more like putty than as a solid. When the drill bit was removed for replacement, the hole tended to flow closed.

As described in Dr. Brown's book, nearly all ancient writings describe a great flood, and worldwide scientific evidence exists to support this theory. The most compelling evidence is the worldwide oceanic ridges and trenches that circle the Earth. (If you look at an online topographical image of the Earth—oceans removed—you will see these ridges and trenches circling the Earth like the seams on a baseball.) If water compressed beneath ten or more miles of Earth's crust is suddenly released, it would have an unimaginable explosive force. The force would be so great that chunks of Earth would be blasted into outer space. The amount of water released might be enough to cover the entire Earth including newly formed mountains. (Perhaps this is why mountains have seashells at their summits.)

Water forced out of ten-mile-deep trench would move land masses apart and cause a global mass imbalance that would result in a rotation of Earth's axis (a pole shift). During this axis rotation process temperate regions would likely become frozen and cause mammoths to freeze instantly in an upright position while eating temperate climate vegetation. The heat generated from the subterranean water explosion would cause granite in the Earth's crust to become like putty and continents to drift apart as a result of water lubrication.

When the continents came to a sudden stop, due to opposing continental movement, the putty-like granite would form mountains. This phenomenon would occur like the buckling of a train when it crashes into another train coming from the opposite direction. After expelling water from the subterranean void, much of the expelled water would, over a long period, recede into a lesser sized subterranean void at a new level about three hundred feet lower than where the ocean level is today. At this reduced level, all of the continents would be connected by land bridges and islands would be accessible by primitive boats. People might then migrate to all parts of the globe.

After reaching its lowest point, the oceans would rise up again to their current level, covering the land bridges and separating the continents. This lowering and subsequent rise of the ocean level would result from water draining into the subterranean void and then being pushed back out again as the Earth's crust settled to fill and compress the subterranean void. Water from large, high-mountain lakes that drained to the lowered ocean level provides a logical explanation of how landmarks like the Grand Canyon were formed.

Occasionally the History Channel has a Noah's ark episode. To their credit, they mentioned the subterranean water theory as one of many possibilities. On the other hand, the theory was followed up with commentary from a geologist who claimed that there is no evidence for subterranean water and that there was no way for this water to have formed. In other words, the History Channel leaves the impression that the subterranean water theory is bogus. The History Channel's geologist also used subliminal terms like biblical myth, Christian fundamentalists, and creationists, to discredit the worldwide flood and the ark, while seeming to present an unbiased, scientifically based program. I wonder if the geologist spokesperson had ever heard about the Kola Superdeep Borehole!

Whether or not God planned to have the flood event happen is a subject of speculation. The Bible implies that God caused the flood to happen because of the evil caused by hybrid humans (Nephilim) and modified humans (Centaurs) that existed in the world at that time. My thinking is that God did not intend to release the *"fountains of the great deep"* when Earth was being terraformed. After all, if Adam had not eaten from the tree of good and evil, there would have been no reason for the destruction of his offspring; in which case, the subterranean water would ooze up and be filtered through ten miles of the Earth's crust to be released on the Earth's surface as a fresh mist to water the ground.[6] This sounds to me like a built-in sprinkler system and source of fresh water for the idealistic Garden of Eden. No rain required. With water separating the Earth's crust from its molten core, it's also conceivable that volcanoes would not erupt, and earthquakes would not occur. With no asteroids or comets resulting from the flood eruption, there would be no chance of their impact with the Earth. In addition, with a uniform global climate and reduced amount of ocean water, the chance of hurricanes, tornadoes, and tsunamis would be less.

---

6   Genesis 2:6 says, "But a mist used to rise from the Earth and water the whole surface of the ground."

Chapter 5—The Mustard Seed Parable

"Then I saw a new heaven and a new earth, for the first heaven and the first earth had passed away, and there was no longer any sea"
Revelation 21:1 NIV

At this point you may be asking, what does all of what I've said so far mean for me personally? Well hang on to your hat, what I'm going to say now could have very important implications that impact all of our lives. If you believe that Jesus Christ was the Son of God, His words will have a profound meaning for you. With that being said, I think the parable of the mustard seed is the most profound of all because it deals with eternal life. In fact, I believe it tells us where we will be going in our afterlife, and what we will do there. More importantly I believe it reveals our very purpose in life, why we were created by God. So, without further ado, let's begin with this passage from the book of

Mathew. When speaking about the Kingdom of Heaven Christ said:

> *The Kingdom of Heaven is like a grain of mustard seed, which a man took and sowed in his field: which indeed is the least of all seeds: but when it is grown, it is the greatest among herbs, and becomes a tree, so that the birds of the air come and lodge in the branches thereof. (Matthew 13:31–32 KJV)*

In this passage Christ is, of course, speaking in a parable, or a story with a hidden meaning. The mustard seed is so small that it takes more than seven hundred seeds to equal one gram, and if one pound equals 454 grams, it's pretty small. Yet, when the seed grows it becomes a tree of significant size.

After hearing about the mustard seed parable in church one Sunday, it reminded me about how insignificant Earth is relative to the universe. I thought of how tiny Earth and its people might be like that mustard seed, and our immortal destiny might be to eventually develop and inhabit the vastness of the universe. This would explain why the universe is so vast.

The pastor's interpretation was that Christ's meager beginning has influenced billions of people throughout the world and will continue to influence more and more people. While this is true, my interpretation goes much further. Although my pastor's view appears to be the view of most theologians, it seems to me that it misses the point Christ is making. After all Christ is speaking about a place called the Kingdom of Heaven, not the process of making a dominant religion here on Earth.

In summary, here is my interpretation. The man sowing a mustard seed must be God. The mustard seed must be planet Earth, and the field must be the universe. Since the mustard seed is so tiny it must represent our insignificantly small (compared to the universe) planet Earth. When the mustard seed (Earth) is planted, it germinates (develops a human population and technologies) and then grows into a tree of significant size. As I see it, the branches of the mustard tree represent places where our immortal souls will go to inhabit the universe. The mustard seed "branches" are places where "birds of the air" (immortal souls) will "lodge" (live) with or without God. How about these places being Kingdoms of Heaven and earthlike planets?

In case you're wondering, an earthlike planet could be a place for those living without God. It could in many ways be described as a place of torment or hell, especially if you were alive in ancient times. Have you ever given any thought to what hell might be like? While much has been written about what heaven might be like, not much has been written about what hell might be like. If we assume that our immortal souls in the Kingdom of Heaven will receive human bodies (possibly with a spiritual body counterpart) why not believe that the souls of non-believers will also receive human bodies? If so, breathing and eating would be an essential part of this even in an afterlife. With that in mind let's review what the book of Revelation says:

> *Then I saw a great white throne and him who sat on it, from whose face the earth and the heaven fled away; and there was found no place for them. And I saw the dead, the great and the small, standing before the throne God;*

> *and books were opened: and another book was opened, which is the book of life: and the dead were judged out of the things which were written in the books, according to their works. And the sea gave up the dead who were in it; and death and Hades gave up the dead who were in them: and they were judged, every man according to their works. And death and Hades were cast into the lake of fire. This is the second death, even the lake of fire. And if any not found written in the book of life, he was cast into the lake of fire. (Revelation 20:11–14 ASV)*

My point in reviewing this somewhat confusing passage from Revelation is that every human who has ever lived will be judged (at the end of the Millennium) by God according to their works (with the exclusion of children and mentally impaired who will probably be admitted into heaven without a trial). Those who are guilty will be sentenced to be cast into the lake of fire (an earthlike planet where the ocean is the lake, and the sun is the fire). The implication is that a varying degree of punishment will be bestowed upon them. Why? Because God's judgement cannot mean that all will receive the same degree of punishment. A person who did not believe in Christ but lives a decent and honorable life, cannot be equated to a mass murderer like Hitler. Thus, the "lake of fire" experience must vary according to a person's works during their human lifetime. Since my mustard seed hypothesis includes newly created earthlike planets throughout the universe being lakes of fire, I can imagine varying degrees of sentencing.

Therefore, the Kingdom of Heaven is a physical place, or places, throughout the universe where believers in Christ reside with God. Their purpose then might be to create branches of the mustard tree (terraformed planets) and most likely watch over and interact with the people living on them. The way they watch over and interact with them could be God's primary purpose for their immortal existence. I'll discuss this in more detail later in this book.

Since our current view of the universe has changed dramatically from what was known more than two thousand years ago, it's now obvious that a seemingly infinite number of solar systems and galaxies exist—and that many other earthlike planets must also exist. However, when I use the term *earthlike*, I don't mean other planets currently exist that are life supporting like our Earth. In other words, planets might exist in the universe that with some modification could be made into life-supporting planets similar to Earth. How about planets like Venus?

As you can see, my "mustard seed parable" hypothesis is more than just a guess. My thinking is strongly influenced by an understanding of today's technology, and how the words that Christ used more than two thousand years ago couldn't be rephrased to reflect what we now know.

As I see it the technologies needed to "branch" out into the universe might be developed during the Millennium (the thousand-year reign of Christ). In fact, it might be the purpose of the Millennium—a time for the technologies needed to accomplish interstellar travel and terraforming. While the spiritual bodies of immortal beings might be capable of instantaneous travel throughout the universe, interstellar movement of physical objects—like robots and construction equipment—would be restricted by the speed of light. After all, if spiritual beings are capable of instantaneous travel to other parts of the universe, what would they find of consequence if not preceded by pre-programmed robotic construction crews that prepare for their arrival?

Another point regarding the Millennium is Adam and Eve's purpose on Earth. It might have been the start of an originally planned Millennium. I say this because coincidentally humans before the flood lived for almost a thousand years. If Adam had not disobeyed God, things could have been totally different. Remember the subterranean water (Noah's flood water)—was a ticking time bomb that went off sixteen hundred years after the creation of Adam and Eve. I can't think of another reason for the Millennium other than to create the technologies needed to "branch" out into the universe.

With the above thoughts in mind, you may be asking what technologies could be developed that could make what I'm saying possible? Let's begin with interstellar travel.

Chapter 6—Interstellar Travel

"And he is before all things, and in him all things hold together."
—Colossians 1:17

After doing the math it quickly became evident to me that it's impossible to carry enough on-board fuel to reach distant solar systems in a reasonable timeframe. The question isn't the propulsion system, since given enough fuel, almost any speed—perhaps up to the speed of light—is achievable. While thinking about this dilemma it occurred to me that steam power plants reuse the same water, and this same idea might work to facilitate interstellar space travel. Let me explain what I mean.

Regarding a steam power plant, water is first heated in a boiler (or steam generator). The steam is then sent to a turbine where it releases its energy in the form of electricity. When the steam leaves the turbine, it has lost most of its energy, and can be condensed back to water and boiled again in a cyclical process. Of course, heat energy is needed to boil the water and cooling energy is needed to condense it. The heat energy for a power plant can come from a nuclear reactor or a natural gas, oil, or even a coal fired boiler. The cooling energy can come from sea water or air—using a cooling tower. Perhaps it's possible that a spacecraft could employ this same principal. As I see it, fusion nuclear energy could be used to either boil the water or split the water into its component parts: hydrogen and oxygen. Interestingly the Apollo/Saturn rockets were fueled by hydrogen and oxygen with the exhaust being superheated steam. Coincidently, high temperature steam will quickly condense by radiation to a dark absolute zero temperature space environment. This loss of energy process simulates the turbine and condenser in a power plant. As a result, the energy in the superheated steam is reduced to freezing water and ice. If this freezing water and ice could somehow be captured and recycled back to the fusion nuclear heating source it could provide a continuous source of recycled fuel that would be limited to the amount of fusion nuclear fuel energy carried on-board the spacecraft. Intrigued by this possibility I began looking at how much fusion fuel would be required for a spacecraft to reach at least a tenth of the speed of light and complete an interstellar mission in a reasonable timeframe. As mentioned in a footnote in the Introduction, 900,000 pounds of helium 3 is enough fusion fuel to provide one year's worth of electric power to support the Earth's current population. Therefore, it seems feasible that enough lightweight helium 3 could be carried on-board the spacecraft in a frozen form to make interstellar travel possible.

My proposed spacecraft would spin to simulate earth's gravity though centrifugal force. Spinning would also provide gyroscopic stability and a means of collecting the water and ice. Although

CHAPTER 6—INTERSTELLAR TRAVEL

what I'm describing has never to my knowledge been proposed by today's mainstream science, I believe it's a workable interstellar travel idea.

―――――

Since no one to the best of my knowledge has proposed my idea, I contacted NASA to get their expert opinion. The following is my response to their letter to me:

Mr. Joe Leopard
Director/Engineering
Marshall Space Flight Center
Dear Mr. Leopard

Thank you for your response to my proposed interstellar travel Idea. Please allow me to respond to each of the points raised by the ACO (Advanced Concepts Office), which are as follows:

1. *The duration of the mission impedes pursuing this technology. The program necessary to successfully carry it out would be too large to sustain the necessary lifecycle costs.*
2. *While the propulsion concepts are impressive, Marshall is already pursuing similar concepts and thus lowering the innovative value of this proposal.*

3. *Although recycling of the spent fuel and oxidizer is intriguing, conceptual feasibility is not possible with currently available materials for the relevant environment being considered.*

My response:

1. *It seems to me that the duration of the mission and life cycle costs is not relevant to my proposal. All I'm asking is for NASA to give a knowledgeable opinion of my concept before I publish it in my forthcoming book. I'm not asking for a NASA program or monetary compensation for my idea.*
2. *I'm not concerned with divulging current NASA programs or the uniqueness of my innovation. All I want is conformation that my idea might be possible in the distant future.*
3. *Thank you for stating that my idea is at least intriguing. If so, it deserves some form of consideration. Are worm holes, ion propulsion, solar kites, and space manipulation feasible? If currently available materials is the reason for rejecting my idea please be specific.*

If my idea has merit (it's "intriguing"), but is limited by currently available materials, why not assume that future materials will be developed? The concept is not based upon materials, it's based upon spent fuel recycling. Please show me why, if a miracle material was available in the future, the spent fuel recycling concept cannot work.

Therefore, based upon NASA's assessment I'm going to publish this concept in my forthcoming book with a footnote stating NASA's opinion. Please provide an update if deemed necessary.

At this point in time I've not received a counter letter from NASA.

So it's conceivable that interstellar space travel is possible. Therefore, pre-programmed self-replicating, nuclear-powered robots could reach distant solar systems as part of a flyby research program. This could prove feasibility and would not endanger human occupants. Although flyby interstellar research will most likely not result in finding life on distant planets, it's something that humans will support because of their innate desire to venture into the unknown.

Let's now see how my proposed design will work for a trip to the Epsilon Eridani solar system, which is 10.8 light-years from Earth. We'll start with a relatively small interstellar spacecraft that might serve as a first step (like the above-mentioned flyby mission) and then explore the possibility of making a huge self-sustaining spacecraft that's capable of transporting a large population. Here is the math supporting my rendition of the small version:

4. *Force = Mass × Acceleration*

5. Velocity = Acceleration × Time
6. Light Speed Velocity = 278,600 kilometers/second
7. A cluster of five Apollo/Saturn rockets have a thrust of about 53 million newtons in space and consume about 13 million kilograms of liquefied hydrogen and oxygen fuel per hour.
8. Converting 13 million pounds of water per hour into liquefied hydrogen and oxygen requires 8 kilowatt hours per kilogram and about 2 kilograms per hour of helium 3 fusion nuclear fuel (remember that nine hundred thousand pounds of helium 3 fuel can power the Earth for about one year—about 2.4×10^{13} kilowatt hours per year).
9. Assume a 1-mile diameter × 1-mile-long interstellar spacecraft has a mass of 12×10^9 kilograms (including fuel) and requires 200 rocket clusters.
10. Two hundred Apollo/Saturn rockets clusters produce a thrust of 10.6×10^9 newtons.
11. Since Acceleration = Force (newtons)/Mass (kilograms), the Acceleration is 0.86 meters/second^2.
12. If we accelerate at 0.86 m/sec^2 for 4 years, we will reach a velocity of 108,156 kilometers / second or 36.34% of light speed.
13. If we coast at 36.34% of the speed of light for 28 years and decelerate for another 4 years, we can reach our destination in about 36 years.
14. Since our water fuel is continually recycled every hour, its onboard mass = 13 million × 200 rocket clusters = 2.6×10^9 kilograms.

15. At 2 kilograms of helium 3 fuel per hour per rocket cluster, 200 rocket clusters require 14×10^6 kilograms in 4 years.
16. Since we are accelerating for 4 years and decelerating for 4 years to reach Epsilon Eridani, and then returning, the helium 3 fuel requirement is 16 years. If we add another 4 years for safety the total is $14 \times 10^6 \times 5 = 70 \times 10^6$ kilograms.

Now let's do the math for a 20-mile diameter × 60-mile long interstellar spacecraft:

1. Assume a 20-mile diameter × 60 miles long interstellar spacecraft has a mass of 3.5×10^{15} kilograms including fuel and requires 100 million rocket clusters.
2. One hundred million Apollo/Saturn rockets produce a thrust of 5.3×10^{15} newtons.
3. Since Acceleration = Force (newtons)/Mass (kilograms) the Acceleration is 1.5 m/sec².
4. If we accelerate at 1.5 m/sec² for 2 years, we will reach a velocity of 94,608 kilometers/second or 34% of light speed.
5. If we coast at 34% of the speed of light for 32 years and decelerate for another 2 years, we can reach our destination in about 36 years.
6. Since our water fuel is continually recycled every hour, its onboard mass = 13 million × 100 million rocket clusters = 1.3×10^{15} kilograms.
7. At 2 kilograms of helium 3 fuel per hour per rocket cluster, 100 million rocket clusters require 3.4×10^{12} kilograms in 2 years.

> 8. *Since we are accelerating for 2 years and decelerating for 2 years to reach Epsilon Eridani, and then returning, the helium 3 fuel requirement is 8 years. If we add another 2 years for safety, the total is 3.4×10^{13} kilograms.*

There are two reasons why I chose the larger spacecraft to be 20-miles diameter and 60 miles long: The first reason is that spinning (to simulate gravity on the inside surface) pre-spacecraft (satellite/habitats) of this size can luxuriously accommodate a self-sustaining population of about 25 million people. With Earth's exponentially growing population, ten thousand of these habitats can accommodate 250 billion people. Considering the quantity of materials available in space (mentioned in the introduction), a population of trillions of people can be accommodated.

The second reason for selecting a spacecraft of this huge size is its potential to combine with other similar sized spacecraft to move an object the size and mass of our Moon. This is precisely how my proposed moon-sized spacecraft can be designed to terraform earthlike planets. However, the specific design will probably surprise you.

What if sometime in the distant future we humans were to develop a means of traveling to distant solar systems and terraform an earthlike planet. If so, we would be viewed by humans living on the terraformed planet as extraterrestrials. Think about it. If the so-called UFOs that are claimed to have been sighted are real, it's conceivable that extraterrestrials on board these UFOs terraformed planet Earth. In which case, Earth's existence could be part of an ongoing process that began whenever. As interesting as this idea might sound, I just don't see it that way. Too many things have happened during Earth's existence that tell me that we are, and will be, the first planet to begin the process of inhabiting the universe. To put it in engineering terms, we are a prototype experiment that was begun by immortal beings (angels) that were created by God before the creation of humans. Lucifer and his followers come to mind.

One important point as to why I believe planet Earth is not part of a previously begun ongoing process, is the life, death, and resurrection of Jesus Christ.

Chapter 7—A Gravity Game

"God doesn't play dice."

—Albert Einstein

For those of you who might be thinking I'm just making up delusional stories to fit my fantasies about God's intent and purpose for our meager existence, I ask that you play a game that I believe will establish mathematical credibility to my proposed thought experiments. The game is easy to play even if you are not mathematically inclined. Because some of the numbers are very large, it would make sense for you to use a spreadsheet like Microsoft Excel.

Here are the equations and some facts that you will need to play this game:

$$F_{centrifugal\,force} = m \times v^2/r \text{ in newtons}$$

m = mass in kilograms

v = velocity in meters per second

r = radius in meters

$F_{gravitational\,force} = G \times m_1 \times m_2 / r^2$ in newtons

G = the gravitational constant 6.67×10^{-11} newton meters^2/kilograms^2

m_1 = the lesser mass in kilograms

m_2 = the greater mass in kilograms

r = radius between gravitational centers in meters

$F_{general\,force} = m \times a$ in newtons

m = mass in kilograms

a = acceleration in meters per second^2

$V_{volume\,of\,a\,sphere} = 4/3 \times \pi \times r^3$ in cubic meters

$\pi = 3.14$

r = radius in meters

$v_{velocity} = a \times t$ in meters per second

a = acceleration in meters per second^2

t = time in seconds

Facts about Venus:

Mass = 4867.5×10^{21} *kg*

Density = *5.243 g/cm^3*

Radius = *6,087,344 m*

Gravity = *8.87 m/sec^2*

Surface temperature = *about 900°F*

Spin rate = *5,832 hours per cycle*

Atmosphere = *carbon dioxide plus other gasses*

Distance from the Sun = *107,531,932,248 m*

Orbit = Near circular
Velocity around Sun = 126,720 km/hour (79,200 mi/hr)

Facts about Earth:

Mass = 5972 × 10^{21} kg
Density = 5.5 g/cm^3
Radius = 6,360,000 m
Gravity = 10.2 m/sec^2
Surface temperature = 58.7°F average
Spin rate = 24 hr/cycle
Atmosphere = 20% oxygen and about 79% nitrogen plus trace gases
Distance from the Sun = 149,674,200,000 m
Orbit = Near circular
Velocity around Sun = 106,000 km/hour (66,200 mi/hr)

Facts about our Moon:

Mass = 72 × 10^{21} kg
Density = 3.34 g/cm^3
Radius = 1,720,000 m
Gravity = 1.6 m/sec^2
Surface temperature = -387°F to 253°F
Spin rate = 655 hr/cycle
Atmosphere = Negligible
Average distance from Earth = 385,000,000 m
Orbit = Near circular (27.3 days to orbit Earth)
Velocity around Earth = 1.022 km/s (2,300 mi/hr)

CHAPTER 7—A GRAVITY GAME

Facts about our Sun:

    Mass = 1988,500,000 × 10^{21} kg
    Radius = 695,700,000 m (434,812 mi)

Facts about Jupiter:

    Mass = 1.8982 × 10^{27} kg
    Radius = 71,492.000 m (44,690 mi)
    Distance from the Sun = 778,547,200,000 m

Facts about our Jupiter's moon Europa:

    Mass = 48 × 1021 kg
    Density = 3.013 g/cm^3
    Radius = 1,561,000 m
    Gravity = 1.314 m/sec^2
    Surface temperature = -276°F average
    Spin rate = 85.2 hr/cycle
    Atmosphere = Negligible
    Distance from Jupiter = 671,000,000 m
    Orbit = Synchronous
    Velocity around Jupiter = 13.14 km/s (29,565 mi/hr)

Here is an example that will help you to get started:

    Calculate Earth's gravity:

$$F_{gravitational\ force} = G \times m_1 \times m_2 / r^2$$
$$G = 6.67 \times 10^{-11} \text{ newton meters}^2/kg^2$$

A DIFFERENT POINT OF VIEW

m_1 = 67 kg (the mass of a person standing on Earth's surface)
m_2 = 5972 × 10^{21} kg (Earth's mass)
r = 6,360,000 m (from Earth's surface to its center)

The result is $F_{gravitational\ force}$ = 659 newtons

Since F = m × a or a = F/m where F = 659 newtons and m = 67 kg, then a = 10 m/sec^2.

Converting meters to feet, we get 32 ft/sec^2 (a number familiar to most people as Earth's gravity).

Now let's play the gravity game where I ask you to calculate the answers to the following questions:

1. *What is the gravitational force between our Earth and Moon?*
2. *The Lagrange point is where a small body of mass is held in a stationary location when the gravitational force between two larger masses are equal. With regard to our Earth, Moon, and Sun, it is the point at which our Moon would assume a stationary position (a stationary eclipse). How far would our Moon be from the Earth when located at its Lagrange point?*
3. *For a moon (or any body of mass) to orbit a planet, its centrifugal force must equal its gravitational attraction force. Our Moon is 381,443,200 meters from Earth and*

traveling in orbit at 1.02 km/s (2,302 miles/hour). If the Moon were moved to an orbit of 28,800,000 meters (14,000 miles from Earth's surface) what would its new velocity be?

4. If Jupiter's moon Europa (which is similar to our Earth's Moon in its size and mass) were a spacecraft that could be located at Venus' Lagrange point, how far from Venus would Europa be?

5. Revelation 21:6 states that the kingdom of Heaven (the new Jerusalem) is 2,400 kilometers in length, width, and depth. If we remove a 2,400-kilometer (1,500-mile) diameter sphere from the center of our Moon, what would the new density of the Moon be?

6. If you were standing on the inside surface of the hollow Moon (as described in question 5), what gravitational force (m/sec^2) would you experience?

If you've done the math correctly, you will have reached some interesting conclusions. Let me explain.

Question 1 – What is the gravitational force between our Earth and Moon?

The answer is 195×10^{18} newtons. This very strong force causes our oceans to have tides and keeps Earth's axis from wobbling out of control. Interestingly, our tidal motion causes Earth to have a varying mass which in turn causes our Moon to move away from Earth at the rate of about 3.8 centimeters (1.5 inches) per year.

Question 2 – How far would our Moon be from the Earth when located at its Lagrange point?

The answer is 253,000 kilometers (158,100 miles) from Earth. This is 63.3% closer than our Moon is now. Our Moon would appear larger to an observer on Earth's surface, the gravitational influence would be considerably greater, and it would block much of the Sun's radiant heat. Note: Since this is my proposed beginning for terraforming our planet, there would not be a problem with disrupting oceans since at this point in the process oceans would not have existed.

Question 3 – If the Moon were moved to an orbit of 22,400,000 meters (14,000 miles) from Earth's surface, what would its new velocity be?

The answer is 4.22 km/s (9,484 m/hr). At this rate of speed, and distance from Earth, the Moon would orbit the Earth in about 7 days rather than its current 27.3 days. The gravitational interaction between the Earth and Moon would be enormous (a force 295 times stronger than it is today). In other words, if the Moon were gravitationally formed 14,000 miles from Earth's surface (after an angled surface collision with Earth—as stated by mainstream science) the Earth's spin rate, atmospheric content, and ocean tide variation would have been greatly affected. Based upon the results of this calculation and no currently observable surface "gashes," the current Earth and Moon angled surface collision theory is untenable. By my logic, the Genesis terraforming account, and supporting arithmetic, indicates that the Moon was, and perhaps still is, a maneuverable spacecraft.

Question 4 – If Jupiter's moon Europa (which is similar to our Earth's Moon in its size and mass) were a spacecraft that could be located at Venus' Lagrange point, how far from Venus would Europa be?

The answer is 166,675 kilometers (104,172 miles). At this stationary location, Europa would almost completely block the Sun and cause Venus to cool. And by now you know the rest of the story.

Question 5 – If we remove a 2,400-kilometer diameter (1,500-mile) sphere from the center of our Moon, what would the new density of the Moon be?

The answer is 5.06 g/cm^3. This is almost equivalent to Earth's density of 5.50 g/cm^3. Mainstream science claims the Moon's density is 3.34 g/cm^3 based upon the assumption that it is solid, not hollow. However, since materials found on the Moon's surface are heavy like titanium, it brings the solid Moon assumption into question. And, as previously mentioned, seismic testing on the Moon showed that it rang like a bell—indicating that it might be hollow.

Question 6 – If you were standing on the inside surface of the hollow Moon (as described in question 5), what gravitational force (m/sec^2) would you experience?

The answer is 9.77 m/sec^2, which is almost equivalent to Earth's gravity. Wow! This is very interesting since people walking on the inside surface would feel like they are walking on planet Earth's surface. Moreover, with an equivalent gravity, oceans and an oxygen and nitrogen atmosphere could develop on the inside surface. Since

I believe God has created everything by design, I wouldn't be surprised to find a miniature sun at the gravitationally neutral center.[7]

In concluding this chapter, consider this quote:

> *When you can measure what you are speaking about, and express it in numbers, you know something about it; but when you cannot measure it, when you cannot express it in numbers, your knowledge is of a meager and unsatisfactory kind; it may be the beginning of knowledge, but you have scarcely, in your thoughts, advanced to the stage of science. (Lord Kelvin, 1883)*

---

[7] Revelation 21:23 says, "And the city had no need for the sun, neither of the moon, to shine in on it; for the glory of God did lighten it, and the lamb is the light thereof." (how about a hollow moon with a gravitationally neutral sun located at its center?)

Chapter 8—Spaceship Moon

"The more I study science the more I believe in God."
—Albert Einstein

Now that you've read about the Venus connection, the mustard seed parable, interstellar travel, and supporting math, I think you will agree that the existence of our Moon is certainly a mystery. As the math described in the previous chapter shows, the Moon could not have been the result of a glancing impact with Earth billions of years ago. The idea of our Moon starting out only fourteen thousand miles from Earth is untenable. If our Moon were located where it is today 4 billion years ago, it would have receded too far away to regulate tides and control Earth's spin axis. In effect it would be unable to support life on Earth today. For our Moon to begin orbiting the Earth as a rouge planet, its velocity and distance from Earth would need to be extremely precise (which is mathematically impossible as a random/uncontrolled happening) in order for it to be captured

A DIFFERENT POINT OF VIEW

by Earth's gravity. With these thoughts in mind, consider these thought-provoking questions about our Moon:

1. *Don't you think it's strange that at this point in time no scientist can positively explain the Moon's existence?*
2. *Don't you think it's strange that if the Moon had a fifteen-hundred-mile diameter sphere removed from its core, that it's density would be close to Earth's density rather than mainstream science's claim that it's 60 percent of Earth's density?*
3. *Don't you think it strange and coincidental that all of the moons in our solar system have a density of about 60 percent of Earth's density? Are they all hollow?*
4. *Don't you think it's strange and coincidental that if the moon had a fifteen-hundred-mile diameter sphere removed from its core that a person standing on the inside surface would experience an earthlike gravity?*
5. *Don't you think it's strange and coincidental that the fifteen-hundred-mile dimension coincides with dimensions mentioned in the book of Revelation for the new Jerusalem?*
6. *Don't you think it's strange and coincidental that our current Moon's size and location forms a perfect eclipse of our Sun, and sustains life on our planet Earth?*
7. *Don't you think it's strange that the Moon's eclipse of the Sun has allowed humans to confirm the fourth dimension of time?*

CHAPTER 8—SPACESHIP MOON

As I see it, based upon these unusual circumstances, the Earth's Moon must have been (or still is) a maneuverable spacecraft. Having a hollow center, that could simulate Earth's gravity on its inside surface, supports the idea that life could exist on this inside surface if a miniature version of our Sun had formed at the Moon's gravitationally neutral center.

Being curious about the possible existence of a mini sun being at the center of our Moon I did further research. As a result, I found that testing during the Apollo 15 and 17 missions showed an outward flow of heat from the Moon's surface of about 20 milliwatts per square meter. After doing the math, it turns out that this heat output is equivalent to the output of 770 gigawatts of power – a mini sun? Could it be that the heat generated from an internal mini sun might be dissipated by design? In other words, does the heat being radiated into space from the Moon match the internal heat generated by an internal sun and results in maintaining a consistent internal temperature? Besides – if the Moon is billions of years old – wouldn't it have cooled by now (especially if it were hollow)?

If all of what I've just said is true, I asked myself, how would people get into and out of a 300-mile (480-kilometer)-thick shell? The simple answer is, boring technology. The same technology used to create the "Chunnel" between England and France would be a logical explanation. With the proper use of airlocks, I can imagine spacecraft traveling back and forth. Are these the UFOs that credible people have claimed to have seen?

If you have been following everything I've said so far in this book, I'm sure you will agree that I have *a different point of view* regarding our Moon. My view sees all that there is as being designed by God to serve a purpose. Certainly, if life does exist inside our Moon, what purpose would that serve? Could it be to house immortal beings (and possibly programable organically designed android helpers)? Could it be that their purpose is to watch over and possibly interact with humans on planet Earth? Could these immortal beings be the angels (think guardian angels) that God created before creating humans? Are these angels capable of taking human form? Were they responsible for the original terraforming of planet Earth in six days? Are they the rogue angels that the book of Genesis refers to as the "sons of god" who mated with human women to create the Nephilim? As one political television news channel stated, **"we report, you decide."** I have reported my thoughts about our Moon, and it's up to you to decide whether I'm right or wrong.

With all of the above being said, the title of this chapter is **"Spaceship Moon."** In which case you may be wondering how a hollow, earth-sized moon could be converted into a spacecraft? To answer this question, I ask that you recall the 20-mile diameter by 60 miles long spinning spacecraft mentioned in Chapter 6. Is it possible for several of these huge spacecrafts to move an earth-sized moon like Europa? The answer is yes, however the question of where these spacecrafts would be attached and how their spinning can be accommodated is not obvious. Are you curious about how I propose doing it?

I'm not going to bore you with more math at this point. Instead, I'll just tell you the results of what I've found. Based upon an assumed central sun in a hollow earth sized moon, I calculated the opposing gravitational forces at an internal Lagrange point for my proposed 20-mile diameter by 60 miles long spacecraft. In other words, my spinning spacecraft could be held in a stationary position (or in orbit) at this location. If ten of these spacecrafts were positioned in a circle and ignited their engines—so to speak—their propulsion force would be orders of magnitude less than the gravitational forces (acting like a magnet) holding them in place at the Lagrange point. As a result, the propulsion force would move an earth-sized moon at an acceleration of about 0.000001 m/sec^2. If this earth-sized spacecraft moon began its transformation as Jupiter's moon Europa, it would be orbiting Jupiter at a speed of 13.14 km/sec, which would give it a fast initial start. In essence it could reach Venus in 1.6 years. It could also reach Mercury in forty-four days after reaching Venus. Using a slingshot effect around Mercury, the speed could be increased or decreased as required.[8]

There you have it—my version of the technology and wherewithal to make a spacecraft moon possible. Not only could it be possible, but my proposed propulsion system would be located inside the hollow moon and thus having no visible external evidence of its capability.

This might be a lot to take in, but let me ask another question. Are there other reasons to support my contention that our Moon is Earth's Kingdom of Heaven? My answer is yes. Notice the wording in the mustard seed parable where the Kingdom of Heaven is described as being *like* a grain of mustard seed. In other words, it's *like* planet Earth but not the same. As a design engineer, I see how the design of planet Earth could be improved

---

8   In orbital mechanics, a gravitational slingshot maneuver, is the use of a planet's gravity to alter the path and speed of a spacecraft.

while maintaining the miraculous good attributes that Earth has. For starters, I would eliminate (or minimize) exposure to cosmic rays and the possibility of being bombarded by asteroids or meteors. Obviously, I would eliminate hurricanes, earthquakes, tsunamis, volcanoes, and flooding. Eliminating certain animals and insects might also be possible, but subject to their interdependencies. Of course, no viruses that are detrimental to human or animal health would exist in my redesign. Could it be that the inside surface of a hollow moon might be the perfect design that God may have created as the Kingdom of Heaven? Could it be that a Kingdom of Heaven will eventually be created in almost every suitable solar system throughout the universe (branches of the mustard tree)?

Wow! I know what you might be thinking. How is it that I am the only person that has thought of this? My answer is that my approach to scientific discovery is different from most scientists and engineers. If you assume—as I do—that everything in the universe is there by design, you begin by asking how would I design it myself? Of course, this line of thinking assumes there was a designer or creator. Besides if other scientists have already thought about what I'm proposing, they may be fearful of disclosing it because it might cost them their careers and livelihoods. At my age, this is not an issue.

As a final point in this **"Spaceship Moon"** chapter, I'm going to add something that I'm reluctant to do. I'm reluctant because all that I've said so far about the Moon being a spaceship is already a stretch of imagination for most people. And, what I'm about to present is a stretch of even my imagination. Consider this unusual Bible verse:

And the sun stood still, and the moon stayed, until the people had avenged themselves upon their enemies. Is not this written in the book of Jasher? So the sun stood still in the midst of heaven, and hasted not to go down about a whole day. (Joshua 10:13 KJV)

If our Moon were to reduce its orbital speed, gravity would take over and cause it to fall towards Earth at a fast rate of speed (similar to a slingshot effect). Because of gravitational interaction between the Moon and Earth, it's conceivable that Earth's spin rate would slow down? If so, an observer on Earth's surface would think the sun had stopped (or slowed) its movement across the sky? Is this a one-time event that actually happened to make this Bible verse valid? As previously stated, **I'm just reporting – you decide.**

Chapter 9—Are We Alone?

"The universe is a pretty big place. If it's just us, seems like an awful waste of space."

—Carl Sagan

THIS QUOTE WOULD MAKE SENSE if one were to look at the way modern-day science sees the universe today. However, this line of scientific thinking has, in my mind, caused many people to believe that there must be other earthlike planets with human-like beings out there. However, from my perspective that wasted space will eventually be filled with the branches of the mustard tree (Kingdoms of Heaven and earthlike planets). Thus, from God's standpoint the universe is not an awful waste of space. It has a purpose.

The question at this point is: could there be other planets like Earth? If so, my "mustard seed parable" hypothesis would be subject to question. So let's explore this possibility beginning with famed Manhattan Project scientist Enrico Fermi who asked, "Where are they?" He asked this question when he and his colleagues were having a side conversation while developing the atomic bomb. Fermi noted that if there are billions of planets in the universe with extraterrestrials that are billions of years more technically advanced than us living on them, they should have contacted us by now. Perhaps we should ask, "Are we alone?" I believe that the existence of planet Earth is a miracle. Too many fortuitous things indicate that a form of intelligence has made Earth possible, and it appears to me that we are alone in the universe, with the exception of God and His angels. Contrary to this premise, I turn to a quote from noted genius physicist Richard Feynman:

> *It doesn't seem to me that this fantastically marvelous universe, this tremendous range of time and space and different kinds of animals, and all the different planets, and all the atoms with all their motions, and so on, all this complicated thing can merely be a stage so that God can watch human beings struggle for good and evil—which is the view that religion has. The stage is too big for the drama.*

This Feynman quote may be interesting and provocative to some people, but it makes one huge assumption: that the universe contains billions of earthlike planets and God can't possibly keep track of them all. It also assumes that God doesn't have helpers—how about angels or "yet to be" immortal beings? Do you believe that there are billions, or even trillions, of earthlike planets? After all, Earth is just a tiny speck in the vastness of the universe, and logic would say that there must be more than one earthlike planet. In my search for the truth and reinforcement of my belief in the existence of God, I've given a lot of thought to the obvious miracles surrounding our tiny planet Earth.

As almost everyone knows, mainstream scientists currently believe that Earth is just one of billions of planets in the universe that can support life. In fact, Dr. Frank Drake, founder of Search for Extra Terrestrial Intelligence (SETI), formulated the Drake equation that predicts the number of these planets. The equation encompassed many variables, such as the number of stars that resemble our sun and the percentage of these stars that may have earthlike planets in habitable zones. The problem with this equation is that it doesn't account for recent scientific discoveries about the uniqueness of planet Earth. So, regardless of how many trillions of planets that exist in the universe, I'll take the contrarian view that there are no other earthlike planets with intelligent life, and if there are, it's because God created them. Or, as my "mustard seed parable" hypothesis suggests, there are Venus-like planets throughout the universe that are waiting to be terraformed. Besides, my "mustard seed parable" hypothesis requires our tiny planet Earth to be the one and only mustard seed that grows and fills the universe. To help validate my reasoning that planet Earth is a unique occurrence, let's examine this possibility.

In his fascinating book *The Case for a Creator*, *Chicago Tribune* columnist Lee Strobel interviews world-renowned experts in the fields of cosmology, physics, astronomy, and biochemistry, to determine whether current science is pointing toward or away from God. As you might suspect, the conclusion was that science is overwhelmingly pointing to a creator God. Strobel's evidence shows scientific information that has emerged over the last fifty years is revealing more and more unexplainable complexity, and the precision by which this complexity is formed can only be attributed to a master designer. The possibility for it to have been formed by random acts of nature is so remote that, to quote a passage from Strobel's book:

> *It would be like throwing a dart from space and hitting a target on Earth that was a trillionth of a trillionth of an inch in diameter.*

Strobel goes on to say that:

> *Earth's location, its size, its composition, its structure, its atmosphere, its temperature, its internal dynamics, and its many intricate cycles that are essential for life—the carbon cycle, the oxygen cycle, the nitrogen cycle, the phosphorous cycle, the sulfur cycle, the calcium cycle, the sodium cycle and so on—testify to the degree to which our planet is exquisitely and precariously balanced.*

Let's begin with Earth's size and location. In a recent American documentary television series entitled *The Universe* the host claimed that in the past, people thought the Earth was the center of the universe; however, we now know that the Earth orbits around the sun rather than the sun orbiting the Earth, and that the sun is just one of billions of suns in the universe. It went on to say the Earth is just an ordinary planet remotely located in an ordinary galaxy. Is this true, though? Is the Earth located in an ordinary location in an ordinary galaxy? The answer is no. Lee Strobel's interviewed famed astronomer Dr. Guillermo Gonzalez—informally known as the "star guy." Dr. Gonzales said:

> *Galaxies have varying degrees of star formation, where interstellar gases coalesce to form stars, star clusters, and massive stars that blow up as supernovae. Places with active star formations are very dangerous, because that's where supernovae explosions occur at a fairly high rate. In our galaxy, those dangerous places are primarily in the spiral arms, where there are hazardous giant molecular clouds. Fortunately, we happen to be situated safely between the Sagittarius and Perseus spiral arms. Also, we are very far from the nucleus of the galaxy, which is also a dangerous place. We now know that there's a massive black hole at the center of our galaxy. In fact, the Hubble space telescope has found that every large nearby galaxy has a giant black hole at its nucleus. And believe me, these are very dangerous things!*
>
> *Most black holes, at any given time, are inactive. But whenever anything gets near or falls into one, it gets torn up by the strong tidal forces. Lots of energy is released, such as gamma rays, X-rays, particle radiation, and anything in the inner region of the galaxy would be subject to high radiation levels. That's very dangerous for life forms. The center of the galaxy is also very dangerous because there are more supernovae exploding in that region.*

CHAPTER 9—ARE WE ALONE?

One more thing: The composition of a spiral galaxy changes as you go out from the center. The abundance of heavy elements is greater towards the center, because that's where star formation has been more vigorous over the history of the galaxy. So, it has been able to cook the hydrogen and helium into heavy elements more quickly, whereas in the outer disk of the galaxy, star formation has been going on more slowly over the years and so the abundance of heavy elements isn't quite as high. Consequently, the outer regions of the disk are less likely to have Earth-type planets.

Now put all this together. The inner region of the galaxy is much more dangerous from radiation and other threats; the outer part of the galaxy isn't going to be able to form Earth-like planets because the heavy elements are not abundant enough; and I haven't even mentioned how the thin disk of our galaxy helps our Sun stay in its desirable circular orbit. A very eccentric orbit could cause it to cross spiral arms and visit the dangerous inner regions of the galaxy, but by being circular it remains in the safe zone. **(Lee Strobel,** Case for a Creator, *2004, pp. 169–70)*

This all works together to create a narrow safe zone where life sustaining planets are possible. First, most galaxies are elliptical rather than spiral. As a result, according to Dr. Gonzales, the contained solar systems orbit their central black hole like a swarm of bees. Because of the wide variation of their travel, they are not conducive to supporting life. The second most abundant type of galaxy is called irregulars, and their solar system randomness is also not conducive to supporting life. Spiral galaxies are the least abundant types, but for various reasons, their variation in size also makes most of them unlikely to support life. This leaves only about two percent of the total number of galaxies with the capability of having an earthlike planet contained within them. Dr. Gonzales said:

> *I've studied other regions—spiral arms, globular clusters, edge of disks—and no matter where it is, it's worse for life. I can't think of any better place than where we are.* (Case for the Creator, *p. 171*)

Regarding recent findings of planets circling other stars, Dr. Gonzales pointed out that most of the orbits were highly elliptical, with only a few being circular. This finding surprised astronomers because they believed other planetary systems would be like ours. The problem with elliptical orbits is that they pose a problem for life. A planet with the mass of Planet Earth would be sensitive to the gas giant planets if they had more eccentric orbits. This would result in making the Earth's temperature variations more dangerous.

If this isn't enough to prove Earth's uniqueness in the universe, consider how perfectly situated Earth is relative to the sun to maintain a watery surface and how Jupiter acts as a space vacuum cleaner to protect Earth from being bombarded by asteroids and comets. And, as Dr. Gonzales points out, our Moon stabilizes the Earth's tilt axis. If our Moon were not there, our tilt axis would swing wildly over a large range and result in major temperature variations. For example, if our tilt axis were close to 90 degrees, rather than its current 23.5 degrees, the North Pole would be exposed to the sun for six months, while the South Pole would be in darkness, then vice versa. Fortunately, the Moon stabilizes the Earth's axis to a variance of about 1.5 degrees.

Then what about our Sun? Is there anything unique about it relative to other suns in the universe? Again, the answer is yes. First of all, it represents ten percent of the most massive stars in the galaxy, which means if you were to pick a star at random, it would most likely be a red dwarf. They are called *red* dwarf stars because they emit most of their radiation in the red part of the spectrum, which makes photosynthesis less efficient. And being that the radiation is mostly in the red part of the spectrum there would be a problem with luminosity. And in order to maintain liquid water on an orbiting planet's surface, it would need to be much closer to the red dwarf star. That would cause a problem with the tidal forces between the star and the planet. They would become so strong the planet would end up in what's called a tidally locked state. This means that the planet always presents the same face towards the star and thus causing unacceptable temperature differences between the lit and unlit sides.

But that's not all. Since the intensity of red dwarf solar flares is about the same as our sun, the particle radiation would be too intense to be conducive to life. Among other things it would strip away an ozone layer. In addition, the lack of ultraviolet radiation would be detrimental to establishing oxygen in a planet's atmosphere. Conversely in the case of more massive stars than our sun, the problem of having excessively high levels of ultraviolet radiation would be detrimental to the formation of life.

With stars more massive than our Sun, the problem, in addition to the higher levels of ultraviolet light, is they don't live as long. Stars just a little more massive than our sun live only a few billion years whereas our sun is expected to last about ten billion years. As a result, everything in the larger star's life cycle happens much faster, like changes in luminosity. Fortunately, our sun is stable in that its light output varies by one-tenth of one percent over its eleven-year sunspot cycle. Besides the stability created by its near circular orbit, the Sun has a high abundance of heavy elements compared to other stars of its age and location within the galaxy. According to Dr. Gonzales, the Sun's metallicity may be near the golden mean for building earthlike habitable terrestrial planets. In the words of Lee Strobel:

> *It would take a star with the highly unusual properties of our Sun—the right mass, the right light, the right composition, the right distance, the right orbit, the right galaxy, and the right location—to nurture living organisms on a circling orbit planet. That makes our sun, and our planet, very rare indeed.* (Case for the Creator, *p. 281)*

Now, what about the size and mass of Earth? Is there anything unusual or unique that should cause us to consider whether or not we are alone in the universe? Again, the answer is yes. First, a terrestrial planet needs a minimum mass to retain an atmosphere. In Dr. Gonzales words:

CHAPTER 9—ARE WE ALONE?

You need an atmosphere for the free exchange of chemicals of life and to protect the inhabitants from cosmic radiation. And you need an oxygen rich atmosphere to support big-brained creatures like humans. Earth's atmosphere is 20 percent oxygen—that's just right it turns out. And the planet has to be a minimum size to keep the heat from its interior from being lost too quickly. It's the heat from its radioactive decaying interior that drives the critically important mantle convection inside the Earth which results in our protective magnetic field. If Earth were smaller, like Mars, it would cool down too quickly; in fact, Mars did cool down and is basically dead. (Case for the Creator, *pp. 180–81)*

More massive planets, according to Dr. Gonzales, would create too much gravitational pull. This would result in a tendency to create a smooth sphere. If Earth were a smooth sphere, our oceans would cover the entire Earth to a depth of about two kilometers and thus creating a water world.

In a water world, tides and weathering would not wash nutrients from continents into the oceans, where they feed organisms. Many of the life-essential minerals would sink to the bottom and the salt concentrations would be prohibitively high. Life can only tolerate a certain level of saltiness. On Earth, salt concentrations are maintained because of marshy areas along some coasts, which through evaporation leaves salt behind. In a water world, excess salt would settle to the bottom and would be inhospitable for life. Besides having a convecting metallic liquid mantle below the Earth's surface causing a protective magnetic shield, a water world could be instrumental in causing heavy elements and ores, essential to the development of human life, not to rise close enough to the surface to allow mining of essential elements.

While I've only touched upon the details supporting the serendipitous, finely tuned requirements and phenomena that established the Earth as a very unique place in the universe, I would like to mention one more very unusual fact: Earth's apparent setup for discovery. Let me begin by asking, don't you think it's strange that when there is a solar eclipse the Moon is the exact same size as the sun when viewed from Earth? It's even more unusual when you consider that, of the nine planets, with sixty-three moons, only Earth's moon provides a total eclipse. Moreover, by providing a total eclipse, Earth's humans have been able to learn about the nature of the stars using spectroscopes to confirm Einstein's theory of relativity by showing that gravity bends light and allows astronomers to calculate the change in the Earth's rotation over the past several thousand years, which is important because it enables us to superimpose ancient calendars on our modern calendar system.

Dr. Gonzales pointed out that the Earth is finely tuned for humans to make measurements that are critical to understanding our universe. His examples include how the Earth is the best overall platform for astronomers and cosmologists to make a diverse range of discoveries. Our location away from the galaxy center and in a flat plane disk provides a privileged vantage point for observing both nearby and distant stars. Because of Earth's tilt, we maintain deep snow and ice deposits, which preserve historical data about the Earth's climate, its early atmosphere, and changes in the Earth's magnetic field. And then there is our atmosphere, which not only provides enough oxygen to sustain life, it also facilitates fire and the development of technology. Furthermore, it just so happens our atmosphere provides transparency, which would not be the case if it contained significant amounts of carbon-containing atoms like methane. A transparent atmosphere has allowed astronomy and cosmology to flourish. Another interesting fact is that movement of the Earth's crust results in earthquakes and other phenomena critical to life. Using seismograph data, scientists have been able to provide a three-dimensional map of the structure of Earth's interior.

So, there you have it, Earth needs to be precisely the right size, mass, and composition. The Moon needs to be precisely the right size and mass, and the Sun needs to be precisely the right size, mass, and composition. In addition, they all need to be precisely located relative to each other, travel in near-circular orbits, and Earth needs to have a large planet nearby to shield it from asteroid bombardment. If that weren't enough, our solar system needs to be located in a specific type of rare spiral galaxy, and at a specific location within that galaxy. With that being said, the conditions on the Earth itself need to be just right to support life and allow for human technological development. If you were to visit another solar system that meets the same criteria, what do you think the odds would be that you would find a planet of just the right size, mass, and composition with just the right sized moon and large nearby planet to shield it from asteroids? Unless they were placed there deliberately, I think that you would agree the odds against finding this rare combination are incredibly high. Needless to say, even if this rare combination were found, it doesn't mean that human-type life will have evolved on the earthlike planet by random natural processes. Given the billions of possible sites in the universe, do all of the above precise earthlike requirements lead to the conclusion that Earth is the only planet of its type in the universe? If the answer is based upon random occurrences, I believe the odds favor Earth being a unique place, especially when you consider recent findings of orbital eccentricity. On the other hand, the unique occurrences themselves strongly indicate that intelligence is behind it all; and if so, that same intelligence could have arranged for many pre-earth planets, such as Venus. Needless to say, the phenomena that supports life and allows for technological advancement of the human species is indeed miraculous in its own right.

Why, through random unguided processes, should we expect to discover an earth-like planets with its stable 20 percent oxygen level and ozone protection? Why, through unguided processes, should we expect to locate a planet with a protective magnetic shield? Why, through unguided processes, should we expect to find a planet with an axial tilt with the same spin rate, that is conducive to stable temperatures, or near-surface ores and elements that have shaped human society, or organic life?

Considering most of scientific teaching today, one might conclude that much of the universe is random in nature and serves no purpose. While in many respects this conclusion appears to be true, let's look at it another way (e.g., **from a different point of view**). While we know that there are billions of known galaxies, and only a small percentage of them are conducive to life, there are still many from a numerical standpoint that are conducive to life. While we know that there are a restricted number of places in each of these inhabitable galaxies that are conducive to life, there are still billions of these restricted places in each of these habitable galaxies. So, does this mean the vast majority of places in the universe are useless, or do they also serve a purpose? My guess is that they do serve a purpose that has yet to be discovered. If nothing else, they may be the result of the natural law requirements for creating the universe.

Chapter 10—God's Cosmic Puzzle

"There are two ways to live your life. One is though nothing is a miracle. The other is though everything is a miracle."

—Albert Einstein

As a child I was interested in piecing puzzles together, figuring out how magic tricks work, and solving riddles. Not surprisingly this attribute has followed me to this day. During my childhood years I would look up into the sky and ask myself where does it all end? After all it's illogical to think of something being infinite. Later in life I discovered that all matter is made up of atoms that are mostly comprised of protons, neutrons, and electrons. If true, I asked myself, what are the protons, neutrons, and electrons made of, and how small can you go? Then there is the mystery of gravity and the forces that hold the atoms together. What are these forces and where do they come from? A mind twister near the top of my puzzle list was learning that time varied with speed and gravity! If that weren't enough, there is the existence of self-replicating life forms, the fortuitous existence of elements and compounds on Earth that are essential to sustaining life, the unusual attributes of our Moon, and then the greatest question of all: what is immortality?

To me, all these facts and questions create what I call a cosmic puzzle. However, I believe God wants mortal humans to solve it. Besides giving us clues in the Bible, He has been giving us other clues for thousands of years, but for some reason our human ability to solve the puzzle has been lacking. Consider this. We humans have been bathed in the Sun's rays for thousands of years, yet it's only in recent years that we have discovered and reproduced nuclear fusion. Planet Earth has been struck by lightning for thousands of years, yet its only now that we've discovered how to generate electricity. Birds have been flying for thousands of years yet it's only in recent times that we have discovered how to fly. The ocean is comprised of oxygen and hydrogen, yet it's only now that we are in the process of using the almost unlimited supply of hydrogen as a means of replacing fossil fuels as the next source of portable energy. Now we humans are exploring space, where additional clues are just now emerging to tell us some amazing things that I believe are more than coincidental.

Although recent technological discoveries may not seem to be part of solving God's cosmic puzzle, I believe they are. I believe this because they comprise an acceleration of technological knowledge that when taken as a whole, can be viewed as having a purpose. As I see it, historical evidence suggests that while God is trying to give us clues to solving the cosmic puzzle, it appears we humans are still having difficulty seeing the forest because there are too many trees in the way.

Considering what I've just said, one has to wonder why God created Adam and Eve and put them in the Garden of Eden without giving them a contemporary home with hot and cold running water and a dishwasher. This then begs the question: why didn't God create robots (or biological androids) and the blueprints needed to create a modern home and a Mercedes-Benz parked in a garage? If God intended the Garden of Eden to be so wonderful, why not go all the way? Does this mean that since God is a spiritual being, technological advances needed by humans need to be created by humans? It's interesting to note, however, that God did provide all of the materials and the wherewithal for humans to invent and create a Mercedes-Benz (and other modern-day conveniences). Are these human inventions and creations part of God's plan? Since God is unquestionably the greatest inventor and creator of all time, it should be a minor task for Him to invent and create a Mercedes-Benz. On the other hand, maybe it's **not** possible. This might explain a lot of things related to our human purpose. Just because God can create life and transform atoms at His command (creating Adam from the dust of the ground), doesn't mean that these transformed atoms can be assembled into an automobile that requires a buildup of supporting technologies, manufacturing plants, an evolving knowledge base, spare parts, mechanics, gas stations, and roads on which to drive. In contrast, the things that God *has* created, baffle human understanding even to this day.

To make my point, allow me to digress for a moment? The last paragraph reminds me of a fictional story about a man who bought some scrubby land and worked hard to transform it into a beautiful garden. He planted trees and flowers in an artistic way. He dug a pond and used some of the leftover dirt, some large boulders, and an electric water pump to create a beautiful waterfall and stream leading to the pond. He designed and built some bridges to cross the stream and blend in with the background. He designed and built swirling walkways to allow visitors to traverse through the garden and see the majestic views. He added some water fountains along with discrete signs that described each tree and plant. He placed benches, shelters, and restrooms at strategic points to allow visitors a place to rest and be protected from an occasional rainfall. Needless to say, all of this was meticulously maintained in a pristine condition. One day as a woman was passing through the garden, the man who created it approached the woman and asked, "How do you like the garden?"

The woman replied, "Isn't it wonderful what God has created?"

The man answered, "You should have seen it when God was taking care of it!"

Don't, get me wrong. God has created some beautiful landscapes accompanied by spectacular sunsets, but humans can, in some cases, use manmade equipment and materials like backhoes, concrete forms, and electric pumps to improve the view. God creates the trees and flowers for man to arrange in creative ways.

The point I'm trying to make is that it appears God needs humans to create the things that humans need or want. If the Kingdom of Heaven is a place (or places), as I see it, then it could very well mean that human technology is needed to construct it (or them). In this regard, God provides the raw materials—like iron ore and trees—for humans to make iron and wooden objects.

A DIFFERENT POINT OF VIEW

The evidence is that God has created the galaxies, suns, planets, moons, and living things, but human technology is needed to transform them for human purposes. Thus, if our immortal afterlife includes a human type of existence, it will logically include human created technologies.

Chapter 11—Our Purpose

"When the solution is simple, God is answering"
—Albert Einstein

IN THE PRECEDING CHAPTERS I have described my thoughts on what God had in mind when He created the universe, planet Earth, and mortal human beings who will live an eternal afterlife. I am not questioning the fact that God exists or that there is an afterlife. I believe these truths are self-evident. What I'm looking for is a coherent explanation for all that there is, what I will be doing for eternity and, more importantly, why.

Let me be clear. I am a churchgoing Christian who has rationalized that Jesus Christ is in fact the Son of God. Although sermons have helped to reinforce my belief, I'm a person who is inclined to look to science and logic for support. For instance, I believe the Shroud of Turin is an authentic image of Christ and that it serves as proof of His divinity. It helps skeptics like me who need scientific validation. After all, wouldn't God want to leave behind a supernatural artifact that would help support what His Son has done for humanity? While the gospel makes sense, it leaves me with questions and counter arguments. However, from a scientific viewpoint, Jesus' spoken words and parables are very compelling. To me the most compelling words spoken by Jesus is the parable about the mustard seed. In my humble opinion, this parable tells me that Jesus knew something about the future that could not have been known by any mortal human of His time. While I may be reading more into the mustard seed parable than it deserves, it has caused me to look for a meaning that is supported by science, other passages in the Bible, and logic.

As I begin my eighth decade of life, I'm giving more thought to my mortality. Since I'm a believing Christian, my main focus is on what am I going to be doing for eternity with God—and why. What is God's plan for us mortal and eventually immortal beings? Am I supposed to play a harp and sing songs of praise to God for eternity, or is there more to it than that? If the answer is to have people worship Him for eternity, I would say thanks for the offer, but could I be excused from participation. On the other hand, if the answer is to allow human souls to experience unimaginable wonders, I would be curious about what these wonders might be. From my experience, eating lobster every day can get old even though I very much enjoy eating lobster. My follow-up question would be, if after experiencing these wonders, will I eventually become bored over an eternity of time? What could be eternally wonderful enough to keep me from becoming bored? Then it occurred to me that I might be given a job that always satisfies.

Genesis chapter 1 says God created everything on planet Earth in six days. After each day God proclaimed that what He had created was good and apparently very satisfying to Him. At the end of the sixth day God rested from the work He had done. Wow! Just think of your own experience of self-satisfaction when creating something useful, completing something worthwhile, reaching a goal, or winning a game. The words "God rested from the work He had done," tells me that we will do creative work for eternity with endless satisfying experiences. This removes the aspect of self-indulgence that experiencing unimaginable wonders might imply. It also removes the aspect of endless worship of God. Don't get me wrong, God is worthy of worship, but I expect that even He doesn't want it on a continuous basis for all of eternity.

Although God is the giver of all that we have, my experience has been to be more satisfied with giving than receiving—especially as I get older. For example, my grandson recently said he really wanted to buy a used car that he liked and planned on saving money to buy it. Although I could afford to buy the car for him, I wanted him to work for the money. I knew from my own experience that he would appreciate the car more if he worked for it. If I had given the car to him, I would have been temporarily happy because it would have made him temporarily happy. On the other hand, he wouldn't have had the satisfaction that comes from working to achieve something he wanted. Similarly, I imagine God saying to Himself, **"I could give human beings everything they desire, but in the long run they would become self-indulgent and dissatisfied."** That is why I see our eternal life as consisting of a type of work that will result in endless satisfactions, and that's where my interpretation of the mustard seed parable might provide some answers.

A DIFFERENT POINT OF VIEW

As a result of writing four books before this one, I discovered some very important things about what I believe to be God's plan. The most notable is the undisputed fact that all we see around us is there by design. Anyone who is familiar with the mathematics of statistical probability would most likely conclude that what we see around us is not possible by random chance. However, I do recognize that some scientists still believe in the notion of random chance and have now adopted the multi-universe theory, which states that given an infinite number of chances, we could get to be where we are. If that's not grasping for straws I don't know what is.

During my many years of life, especially during my engineering career, I've been a maverick. In other words, I don't, and never have, followed the crowd—or the party line. Whenever I hear a consensus opinion, I tend to be skeptical. Thus, I'm not a joiner or a person who goes along to get along. I question almost everything. Perhaps after having read this book, you have come to realize just how much of a maverick I am. However, one thing that has resulted, after many years of skepticism, is my current belief that the Old and New Testaments of the Bible are literally true.

While it's true that God's wording in the Bible can't be improved, it's not true that new interpretations of God's words aren't valid. The problem is that new interpretations are generally met with scorn because of what people have been conditioned to believe. So, from that standpoint I shouldn't have written this book. On the other hand, people who have read this book with an open mind may have found some intriguing new thoughts that will spark their imagination and further their understanding and belief in the Bible. In fact, since this book deals with what we might be doing in our afterlife, it may be of interest to people like me who are searching for answers to this question.

By reading between the lines of the Bible I'm not contradicting it; instead, I'm trying to explain it—especially to myself. While many people don't believe in the literal six days of creating planet Earth, I would ask why then should you believe the rest of the Bible? While what you have read in this book may seem outlandish and farfetched from your perspective, just keep in mind, I'm not contradicting the Bible.

Chapter 12—Concluding Remarks

"No one can read the gospel without feeling the actual presents of Jesus. His personality pulsates in every word."

—Albert Einstein

I'M SURE MANY OF YOU who have read this book disagree, and are perhaps shocked, with what I've proposed. In fact, I considered not publishing it at all. If on the other hand this book has helped you in some way, I'm happy to have made that possible. Moreover, if you were not a Bible believing Christian before reading this book, but now you are a Bible believing Christian, I'm more than happy about that.

If you believe that we humans have immortal souls that go to another place after we die, there needs to be an explanation for what that place might be and what we will do when we get there. Of course, the Bible is the only place to find answers to these profound questions. But because the Bible was written in terms that fit what was known at the time it was written, I believe an updated interpretation is needed to fit our current knowledge. As I see it, the Bible's wording probably needs what will be known at a future point in time to fully understand what is being said. By predicting what may happen in the future, I've discovered some amazing things that have surprised me. After taking into account that everything in the universe is there by design, especially after doing some math for validation, a whole new range of possibilities has been opened up to me.

The idea of immortal souls having human-like bodies and going to a physical place (or places) is biblical. Since these physical places will require air, food, and water it begs an important question: Are these places primitive gardens of Eden or do they include man-made structures? If they include man-made structures, logic would say that they will require humans (or programmable robots or androids) and processed materials to construct them. As stated before, God doesn't make man-made structures. Instead, He provides the wherewithal (like iron ore and trees) to make them. Continuing with this thought, current man-made structures generally require man-made technologies and equipment, like electricity and bulldozers. Thus, our current and future technologies will play an important role in the place or places we will go to in our immortal existence. While our immortal bodies might have a spiritual aspect to them that allows travel to any place in the universe in the blink of an eye, the speed of light limitation for physical objects requires a man-made high-speed transportation system. Therefore, my guess is that remote controlled robotic systems will travel to locations throughout the universe in advance of the arrival of immortal beings. These robotic systems could be programmed to construct physical man-made places for immortals to reside when they arrive. If this were not true, when an immortal travels to anyplace in the universe—in the blink of an eye—he or she would at best end up in a primitive Garden of Eden type of place. On the other hand, if immortal beings were not capable of traveling throughout the universe in the blink of an eye, our immense universe would serve no purpose, in which case, my contention that everything in the universe is there by design would need to be reassessed.

Now we come to the question of who goes where and why? In other words, since the souls of all human beings are immortal, where do these immortals go and what determines why they will go there. Since the Bible says all humans will be judged by God based their works at the Great White Throne—at the end of the Millennium—their destination will be determined by God. Again, referencing what the Bible has to say about their destination, it says:

> *Then I saw a great white throne and Him who sat on it, from whose face the earth and the heaven fled away. And there was found no place for them. And I saw the dead, small and great, standing before God, and books were opened. And another book was opened, which is the Book of Life. And the dead were judged according to their works, by the things which were written in the books. The sea gave up the dead who were in it, and Death and Hades delivered up the dead who were in them. And they were judged, each one according to his works. Then Death and Hades were cast into the lake*

of fire. This is the second death. And anyone not found written in the Book of Life was cast into the lake of fire. (Revelation 20:11–14 NKJV)

In this regard I imagine everything we humans have done and will do is recorded in the hard drive portion of our biological computer brain and uploaded to God and His helpers for evaluation and judgement at the time of our death. I've heard that at the time of death a person's life flashes before their eyes. Perhaps this is an upload event that is triggered just before death.

Since judgement by God generally means evaluation and sentencing, the implication is that our sentencing will be based upon our works, and that applies to those who believe in Christ too. Just because you accepted Christ during your lifetime and had your prior indiscretions forgiven, doesn't mean that unrepented indiscretions after your acceptance of Christ won't be evaluated and sentenced in some way. In God's kingdom there is most likely a hierarchy where the worst offenders—those who have not repented of their indiscretions after belief in Christ—will be on the lowest rung of a hierarchy ladder. As I see it, those who did not accept Christ during their lifetime will be evaluated and sentenced according to their entire lifetime of works. Since there are people who lived prior to the arrival of Christ, others who have never heard the gospel, and those who rejected Christ after hearing the gospel, I can only assume that those with the least offensive indiscretions will have a last-minute chance to be admitted into God's kingdom. How about the person who died on the cross next to Christ who was admitted to the Kingdom of Heaven?

The Bible says **"I am the way and the truth and the life. No one comes to the Father except through me"** (John 14:6 NKJV).

Therefore no one is admitted to the Father except through Jesus. But, since Jesus will judge all humans who ever lived, at the Great White Throne, it's logical to believe that their lifetime of works can get them into heaven if they accept Jesus at this trial and repent of their lifetime of indiscretions. Although this idea runs counter to current Christian teaching, it's what I believe because there must be a way for pre and post Christian mortals (before and after Christ's appearance on Earth) to be admitted into heaven. As you can see from Revelation 20, excerpted above, if you read between the lines, you will stand before Jesus (or those chosen to represent Him). Therefore, as I see it, you will have a last-minute chance to repent and enter God's Kingdom—through Jesus.

On the other hand, others will be sentenced to live in a lake of fire:

> *But as for the cowardly, the faithless, the polluted, the murderers, the fornicators, the sorcerers, the idolaters, and all liars, their lot shall be in the lake that burns with fire and sulphur, which is the second death. (Revelation 21:8 NRSV)*

My logic says that not all of those sentenced to the lake of fire will experience the same degree of torment. Why? Because sentencing must by definition fit the crime. For instance, a mass murderer like Hitler might be sentenced to slave labor building pyramids in the equivalent of ancient Egypt, while a nonbelieving Christian, who has led a good and honorable life, might experience the equivalent of a twenty-first-century life in America. Moreover, since sentencing usually has an expiration date, it's reasonable to assume an eventual release into God's kingdom (probably at a lower hierarchical level).

Regarding the above-mentioned passage from Revelation, a second death must also mean a second mortal birth. Furthermore, since we are talking about eternity, it appears that the implication is continual rebirths and deaths. My take is that there is only one second death, and at that time you will have served your term and will enter the Kingdom of Heaven. On the other hand, the words a "second death" might also mean exactly what it says—no more immortal life, or your immortal life might be held in a non-existent state (like at zero time).

My thinking is that all the souls that are cast into the lake of fire are still given a chance to repent and enter God's kingdom. Consider the story of the prodigal son.

A father has two sons. The younger son asks the father for his inheritance, and the father grants his son's request. However, the younger son is prodigal (i.e., wasteful and extravagant) and squanders his fortune, eventually becoming destitute. The younger son is forced to return home empty handed and intends to beg his father to accept him back as a servant. To the son's surprise, he is not scorned by his father but is welcomed back with celebration and fanfare. Envious, the older son refuses to participate in the festivities. The father tells the older son, **"you are always with me, and all that I have is yours, but we had to celebrate and rejoice, because this brother of yours was dead and has begun to live, and was lost and has been found"** (Luke 15:31–32 NASB).

While many Christians believe that being cast into the lake of fire means eternal torment, I believe that idea is false since the Bible does not exclude repentance as a form of release from torment.

So, there you have it: my version of what will happen during our immortal lives. Although my thoughts run counter to current Christian teaching, I believe the Christian religion has suffered and declined because many non-Christians believe it to be exclusionary, and don't believe that a loving God would sentence non-believers to an eternal life of torment. In this regard, I believe Christianity needs a face lift. By reading between the lines of the Bible—in modern-day terms—perhaps Christianity needs a new reformation and revival. On the other hand, perhaps God has a plan to fix the problem more directly. How about the rapture, tribulation, and Millennium? If so, from what I'm now seeing, the tribulation may have already begun.

When looking at the big picture, so to speak, we may see our human experience as a means by which God is dealing with a free will that has the ability to choose evil. Since the results of evil has been on display on planet Earth since its inception, it serves as a history lesson for immortal beings who have been accepted into God's kingdom. Thus, God sent His son Jesus to serve two purposes. The first purpose was to cause humans to change their lives by voluntarily rejecting evil after accepting Christ. The second purpose was to demonstrate that life continues after death. It appears then that by accepting those that reject evil into the Kingdom of Heaven, God is solving the free will/evil problem. I believe the Kingdom of Heaven can be described as a place of unlimited exploration that might include visiting trillions of earthlike places throughout our vast universe. It might also include experiencing great food, music, sporting events, and relationships. We might also be capable of traveling forward and backward in time and creating things like houses, landscapes, and perhaps living creatures. But, as I see it, our ultimate goal and work as immortals might be to bring as many condemned immortal beings into God's kingdom as possible. The apostle Peter wrote:

> *But, beloved, be not ignorant of this one thing, that one day [is] with the Lord as a thousand years, and a thousand years as one day. The Lord is not slack concerning his promise, as some men count slackness; but is longsuffering to us-ward, not willing that any should perish, but that all should come to repentance. (2 Peter 3:8–9 KJV)*

Thus, our work as immortals might be a form of competition that has rewards like moving up in a hierarchy ladder that approaches the capabilities of God. The work of bringing condemned beings—living on earthlike planets—into God's kingdom is probably part of God's ultimate goal. I believe that this is God's way of dealing with beings who have a free will and who have chosen evil. As I see it, it doesn't take a genius to see the heartache and torment that not following God's rules have caused people throughout Earth's history. This heartache and torment will be continually on display in various forms on other "lakes of fire" earthlike planets as they are being created throughout the universe.

Finally – consider this:

> *I will surely bless you, and I will multiply your descendants like the stars in the sky and the sand on the seashore. Your descendants will possess the gates of their enemies. (Genesis 22:17)*

Astronomers have estimated that the number of stars in the known Universe to be 70×10^{21}. A further estimate indicated that the number of grains of sand on every beach and desert on Earth is about ten times less than this number. Wow —God knew that the number of stars in the sky and grains of sand on our seashores was a logical comparison when this verse of the Bible was written thousands of years ago. More importantly – it's obvious that planet Earth could not accommodate a population this great (Earth's current human population is about 7.5×10^9), but the universe can! Does this mean that our immortal life will include terraforming earth-like planets throughout the universe?

About the Author

Mr. Bongaards' degree is in mechanical engineering from Northeastern University. Upon graduation, in 1964, he was commissioned a lieutenant in the United States Army and served in Vietnam.

In August 1966 he began his career with the Westinghouse Electric Corporation. During that time, he worked on nuclear steam generator development and was eventually promoted to Section Engineering Manager and later, Department Engineering Manager.

In 1982, he transferred to the Thermo King Corporation (a subsidiary of Westinghouse) to become Engineering Manager for the Truck Transport Refrigeration Equipment Department. During that time, he was given responsibility for design engineering activities at Thermo King factories in Barcelona, Spain; Hamble, England; and Prague, Czech Republic.

Mr. Bongaards has written numerous technical papers for international conferences and for the American Society of Mechanical Engineers (ASME), and currently holds seven patents. He became Chairman of the Florida West Coast Section of ASME in 1974-75 and passed the State of Florida professional engineering examination in 1975. This is the fifth book that he has written since retirement.

www.ingramcontent.com/pod-product-compliance
Lightning Source LLC
Chambersburg PA
CBHW021448070526
44577CB00002B/311